C000017904

Once Upon a Line ...

The ornate signal gantry at the end of the 'down' platform at Ryde St John's Road station shows the line clear for Driver Jim Stone to open up the regulator of Class O2 0-4-4 tank No. 25 *Godshill*, which is departing with a summer service train for Newport and Cowes.

R. J. Blenkinsop

Half title: **O2 class 0-4-4Ts Nos 17 *Seaview* and 26 *Whitwell*** on the 9.20am to Ventnor pictured here at Wroxall station on 10th July 1965. Double heading south of Shanklin was very unusual which makes this picture quite out of the ordinary.

John Goss

Once Upon a Line...

Andrew Britton

Oxford Publishing Co.

Foreword
by R.J. 'Dick' Blenkinsop

I was lucky enough to see the last few years of steam operation on the Isle of Wight as we started taking our annual holidays in the Island in 1961 and have done so ever since. To the railway photographer the Island Railways were a dream and it mattered not that the motive power came from virtually one proven class of locomotive. It was sad that I missed the Freshwater line although I travelled on it in 1936 when visiting Carisbrooke Castle and also a through train, if I remember correctly, in 1949 from Cowes to Ventnor West.

But all this is in the past, and we just have the earthworks left of the forgotten lines to search for amongst the undergrowth. Fortunately the Isle of Wight Steam Railway is a hive of activity at Haven Street and towards the west and soon to expand in the other direction to a new link at Smallbrook Junction.

I have been involved with Andrew Britton's first two volumes of *Once Upon a Line* and it has been a fascinating story to be continued in this latest book, for which I have been asked to pen a few notes. Many is the time when he has come back

from the Island with new stories told to him by people who worked on the Railway and he has telephoned to let me know of some new discovery – or was it that he had to share his news with someone in the district? I am not sure how many times he has been down to the Island and how many interviews he has conducted, but the results are here for all to see and enjoy.

Many are the history books and photographic albums produced on the railways of Great Britain but these three volumes by Andrew Britton are very different, as they deal with the people who worked on the Railway and how it was part of their everyday life.

I am delighted to have been a very small part of this original approach to railway history and would like to say on behalf of you the reader a thank you to Andrew for making it all possible.

Driver 'Ginger' Minter's view from the spectacle of No. 14 *Fishbourne*, prior to departure from Ryde Pier Head on 5th August 1966.

G. S. Cocks

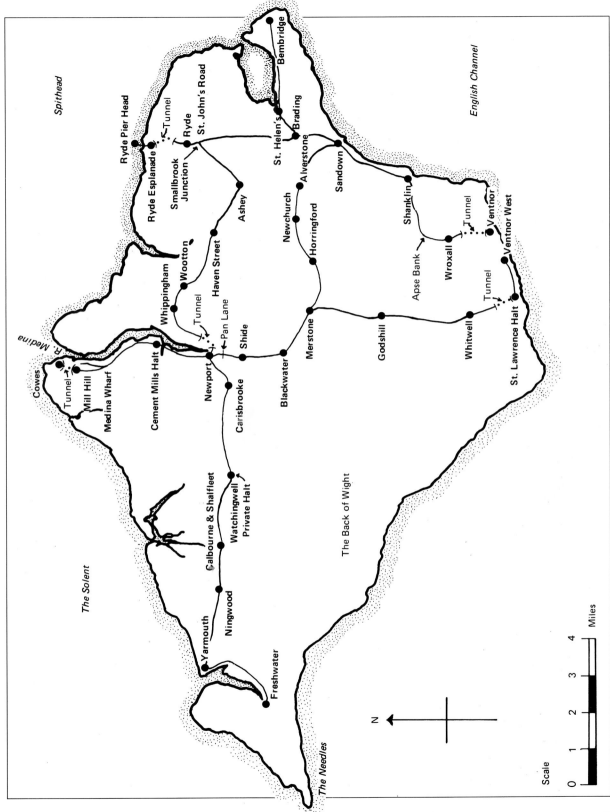

Spithead

English Channel

Ryde Pier Head
Ryde Esplanade
Smallbrook Junction
Tunnel
Ryde
St. John's Road
Bembridge
Brading
St. Helen's
Alverstone
Sandown
Ashey
Newchurch
Horringford
Shanklin
Wootton
Apse Bank
Whippingham
Haven Street
Ventnor
Tunnel
Wroxall
Ventnor West
Tunnel
Pan Lane
Shide
R. Medina
Merstone
Godshill
Newport
Blackwater
Whitwell
Cement Mills Halt
Carisbrooke
St. Lawrence Halt
Tunnel
Mill Hill
Medina Wharf
Cowes
The Solent
The Back of Wight
Calbourne & Shalfleet
Watchingwell Private Halt
Ningwood
Yarmouth
Freshwater
The Needles

N

Scale
0   1   2   3   4
Miles

7

Preface

On the day of publication of *Once Upon A Line Volume Two*, a special launch for the book was held at the Isle of Wight Steam Railway at Haven Street. In conjunction with the book's launch, I organised a reunion of former Island railway staff who were treated to a steam hauled ride to Wootton and return. On arrival back at Haven Street, I was asked by Owen Attrill to consider the possibility of producing another book of Island railway staff reminiscences to include those left out of the two previous volumes. Not imagining that it would be possible to find enough new material for another book, I was surprised to discover that there was an abundance of fresh information and photographs.

The research of material and actual writing of this book has taken considerably longer than at first anticipated, as the former Island railway staff interviewed have long since moved away from the Isle of Wight to parts far and wide. Thus actually tracing and contacting contributors of this book has therefore proved geographically difficult. In addition to this factor during the period of research, my wife was taken seriously ill, but has thankfully made a full recovery. My family and friends: Dick Blenkinsop, Richard Newman, Jimmy James, Ken West and Owen Attrill have encouraged me enormously. Indeed Owen Attrill and Richard Newman have opened their homes to me with five star food and accommodation.

Without doubt one of the major points of interest in *Once Upon A Line Volume Two* was the contribution of illustrations and cartoon drawings produced by Jimmy E. James. Their inclusion not only delighted Island railway staff and enthusiasts, but they were highly acclaimed in press reviews of the book. Today, these James original illustrations are greatly sought after and have proved to be extremely popular with railway enthusiasts and non-railway enthusiasts alike. Many requests have been received for the inclusion of more of Jimmy James' unique work and I am pleased to say that Jimmy has produced a further selection of his art work.

Sadly, since commencing work on this project several of the contributors have passed away. It is my hope that their memories will live on in these pages to keep alive in others an enthusiasm for steam on the Isle of Wight. At the request of the late Vic Hailes, the former signalman of Smallbrook Junction, this book is dedicated to "All the wives and families who have supported and continue to support those involved with railway work".

Ryde shed's O2 class tank No 20 *Shanklin* complete with original mainland bunker at Ventnor. The Ryde crew are Driver Bill Hayward on the right and Fireman Jack Bradford on the left.
George H. Hunt

Chapter One – Stories of the Footplate
(Including an account of the last steam hauled passenger train.)

Harry 'Toby' Watson

After reading through *Once Upon A Line Volume One* and browsing through my contribution some more memories came to mind.

We were shunting one December evening outside Newport paintshops. I saw some lights in the workshops and we then heard some explosions. Upon closer inspection we saw that it was a fire. By breaking some glass, I was able to climb in and by using an extinguisher I put the blaze out. A year later I was called up to Waterloo where I was presented with an award, sealed in an envelope as a token of recognition of my assistance. The citation read that I had managed to save the 300 ft long workshops, six carriages, a stack of timber and the paint store with a total value of £5,000. Enclosed was a cheque for a mere one pound! Upon return to Newport shed, Mr Bell the Foreman enquired if I had been treated well. I replied, "Yes, Mr Bell – so well that the next time your workshops are on fire they can burn to a cinder!"

As mentioned in the earlier book my career dates back to the Isle of Wight Central era. I remember a notable incident during this period at Newport station, whilst I was waiting for the next turn of duty on a little Brighton "Terrier" tank. A young porter called Arthur Hayter was collecting the tickets from passengers who had arrived on a train from Ventnor West and Merstone. In those days, season ticket holders went through one exit and the remaining ticket holders through another. Now Arthur's job was to check the season tickets and he stopped a solicitor whose yearly first class season ticket was out of date. The solicitor then demanded to see Mr Russell Wilmott, the General Manager. The boss then called the young porter and solicitor up to his office. After the situation had been explained to Mr Wilmott he proceeded to reprimand his young porter and stated that he would be fined eighteen pence at the end of the week for insolence to a first class passenger. Arthur then came down the stairs and tried to console himself on my engine footplate. A few minutes passed and the internal station whistle communicating device sounded "This is Mr Wilmott. Send Hayter up to me at once." Arthur Hayter duly returned up to Mr Wilmott's office expecting more trouble. This time however the General Manager apologised for his actions and explained that the first class passenger was a personal friend, and he had to do something about it. He informed Arthur that he could forget the fine and that as recompense for his trouble a wage increase of sixpence a week would be paid to him.

In *Once Upon A Line Volume Two,* Mrs Katie Buckett refers to an incident that occurred at Calbourne station, when a lady fell under a train. I can confirm that the account of the incident is true and I can add more detail from my own memories. As I recall it was a wet and windy night, a real south westerly gale blowing. The lady passenger was a regular passenger on the last train from Freshwater. On this particular occasion the two coach train was hauled by a Brighton "Terrier" tank driven by Driver Jack Sewell. The lady alighted from the train and crossed over the line via the crossing, in

E1 class No. 2 *Yarmouth* speeds bunker first towards Smallbrook Junction with a train of four-wheeler carriage stock, bound for Newport and Cowes.

J. R. G. Griffiths

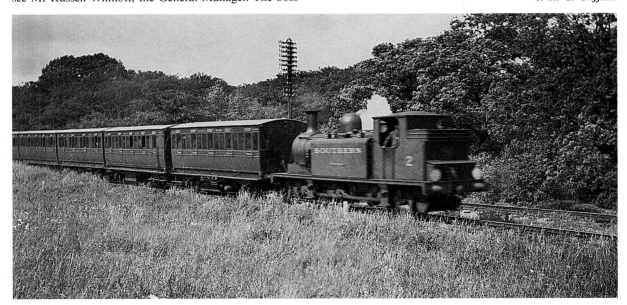

front of the engine. At this point she put up her umbrella but the wind dragged her up the line, in between the rails. Meanwhile, Jack Sewell, who was given the "right away" opened the regulator on his engine and set off towards Newport unaware of what had happened. It was not until he arrived at Newport station that the remains of the umbrella were discovered on the front of the locomotive. I can also confirm that the locomotive and two carriages drove straight over the lady passenger who laid in between the lines, and how she escaped injury of a more serious nature defies belief!

Just after the Second World War there was another

Above: **Fireman Ray 'Joey' Maxfield is pictured shovelling coal into No. 24 Calbourne's firebox as the locomotive ascends Apse Bank in 1966.**

Rod Hoyle

Right: **Driver Ken West (right) hands over the single line token hoop for the Smallbrook Junction to Brading single line section, to his regular fireman Ray 'Joey' Maxfield on the footplate of the now preserved No. 24 Calbourne, in 1966. Later on in the day Driver West and Fireman Maxfield played host to Tim Webb, Andrew Britton and his father. The two boys spent many happy hours sitting on the engineman's lockers in the cab of No. 24 watching the footplate crew in action.**

Rod Hoyle

Miraculous escape from fatal injury on the Freshwater line. Driver Charlie Harvey was at the controls of O2 tank No. 30 *Shorwell.* Approaching Calbourne Viaduct Driver Harvey spotted a tractor and trailer stuck on a farm crossing near Dowty's siding. Two young girls were in charge of the tractor and trailer. One girl had opened the farm gate and waved her companion on over the crossing without even bothering to look. Now back on the engine Charlie Harvey sounded the whistle for all he was worth and applied the Westinghouse brakes fully, but the O2 tank hit the tractor and knocked it over. The diesel oil sprayed all over the rails causing the engine to slip and slide. The land girl who was driving the tractor was flung up into the air and landed on the buffer beam of the engine and somehow she only sustained minor cuts and bruises. What a lucky girl she was.

Ken West

Although most of my reminiscences are recorded in *Once Upon A Line Volume One,* more memories have come to mind since the publication of that book. I therefore welcome this opportunity to recall some more anecdotes of life behind the scenes on the Island railways.

Just after I came out of the Army in 1947, when firing to Driver Bill Bishop on engine No. 29 *Alverstone,* I recall a rather amusing incident occurring at Freshwater. We worked the first train of the day from Newport to Freshwater which was a mixed train of carriages and wagons with a brake van. We uncoupled the brake van before entering Freshwater station, as was the practice, and proceeded to complete the normal shunting movements after leaving the carriages in the platform line. As dawn broke and the sun rose, Driver Bishop asked me if I could spot the brake van. We looked all around,

but it was not there. Next, we asked our guard Herbie Fallick where the missing vehicle was. What had happened was that the van had not had its handbrake screwed down and consequently it had run down the slight gradient from the water column to finally come to a halt at Causeway Crossing gates. We made our way down on No. 29 to the gates and low and behold there it was just resting on the gates, but luckily no damage caused.

Although No. 24 *Calbourne* was later my regular engine, I always loved to work on No. 1 *Medina* which was the most powerful locomotive of the four E1 class 0-6-0 tank engines based on the Isle of Wight. We all reckoned she was stronger than the other three put together. The only regular problems I ever encountered with this type of engine was when working the through Ventnor–Freshwater "Tourist" train. This particular train ran from Mondays to Fridays and the journey time allowed was 67 minutes. On Saturdays it had originally run from Sandown, but later Ventnor became the starting point. A four-set bogie coach train was usually used, together with the Island's two bogie saloon coaches. The practice was to have the train hauled by an E1 between Ventnor and Newport and an O2 for the remainder of the journey to Freshwater. It was at the change over point at Newport station where we experienced problems. When the O2 locomotive took over there would often be trouble with the brakes as the E1 class carried an additional ten pounds of pressure.

The only time I really experienced problems with an E1 was whilst firing to Driver Ted Joyce on No. 3 *Ryde*. We were working a mixed train composed of 19 coal wagons, which included several 13 ton wagons, plus three passenger coaches and a brake van. Our aim was to work this evening freight train to Ryde St John's Road where we would be relieved, thus allowing us to catch a connecting Ryde–Newport–Cowes service train home immediately. Any delay would mean an hour-long wait for the next service train back to Newport. Heading out of Newport across the curved viaduct Ted opened No. 3's regulator 'wide open' through the short tunnel and up Fairlee bank. Ted turned to me and said, "She's not going to get up here, mate. Come and give me a hand, I've got an idea". I took hold of the regulator while he caught hold of the reversing lever. He had a cunning plan to shut the regulator, drop the lever down a couple of nicks and then quickly re-open the regulator wide. This would keep the momentum going and give us more power. Unfortunately, things did not go to plan as the lever jumped out. Ted still kept going and was determined not to be beaten. Number 3 struggled up past Mews Lane crossing, through Whippingham station where our pressure was 110 lb per square inch, and she gave her all up the 1 in 64 climb to Wootton. Eventually, we came to a dead stop at Wootton station right on the curve. 'This is it now', I thought, 'We'll have to get some assistance'. Driver Joyce would still not show the white flag and he sent me back to the guard with details of his next plan of action. When I returned to the footplate of *Ryde*, Ted Joyce had built up so much steam her safety valves were lifting. Ted then put his plan

to the test. The guard had screwed down his brake and Ted let the E1 drop back in reverse into the train. This action acted as a cushion effect and the buffers sprang back to push us forward. At this precise moment Ted opened her up and away we went non-stop to Ryde. The time lost however meant that rush as we did, at speeds of up to 50 mph, we still failed to meet out connection for the return trip to Newport.

Ted Joyce and I had another near squeak one day out on the Ventnor West branch. We were waiting at Newport aboard a spare engine, No. 26 *Whitwell,* and as we looked out of the cab we marvelled at the height of the snow. It was a particularly bad winter in 1947 and the Island suffered quite severely from the heavy fall. Presently, we were summoned to Godshill where Driver Harold Lacey was stuck fast in a wall of snow whilst working a one coach push-pull train from Merstone to Ventnor West. His little Brighton "Terrier", which was either No. 13 *Carisbrooke* or No. 8 *Freshwater,* had run its tanks dry. We therefore hauled the locomotive and coach back to Merstone and took over this turn of duty. Ted's ploy on our O2 tank *Whitwell* was to hit the snow drifts at speed.

When we were stopped, Ted would throw the engine into reverse and have another go. Everything was white in the surrounding countryside and I became slightly worried about getting stranded ourselves. Nevertheless, Ted pushed *Whitwell* all the way through to Ventnor West. It was a good job that men from Newport shed were working this turn – had it have been Ryde shed men they would have given up and gone home!

One special person who must have a mention is Driver Frank Ash. He was one of the best locomotive drivers on the Isle of Wight, who sadly passed away before he could make a contribution of his reminiscences in his own right.

Frank commenced work at Newport shed mid-way through the Second World War in 1942, and climbed the ladder in the traditional style from cleaner to fireman and eventually driver. His regular engine was No. 18 *Ningwood,* once the pride of Ryde shed. Being on the short side, his leg was often pulled about standing on a box in order to see out of the locomotives spectacle windows, but this made no difference to Frank's capabilities when at the controls of his *Ningwood*. His railway work was all part and parcel with his domestic life at home, as he married June Prangnell who was the daughter of Harry Prangnell of Newport station. Naturally enough, this keen and dedicated railwayman even lived in a railway station at Blackwater on the Newport-Sandown line. Many an off duty nap was disturbed by his footplate colleagues blowing their engine whistles outside his bedroom window. In fact, Frank used to say that he thought the train was coming through the front room.

Living in a station property had its good points, but many a morning Frank was called from his bed to open and close the crossing gates for the passage of a train owing to the early turn porter not having arrived for duty. A favourite trick of footplate crews with trains stopping at Blackwater when running in bunker first, was to lift the safety valves, thus spraying water all over the place. This was a regular occurrence on wash days. To make matters worse, a few black smuts from the Drummond O2 chimney, especially on the sheets and nappies made Frank's life miserable, with Mrs June Ash having double the work load! Any anguish was short lived and a nice hot cup of tea and biscuits was appreciated by crews when shunting at Blackwater sidings.

Unless the locomotive failed through mechanical difficulties, Frank's *Ningwood* was always right on time and this custom continued when he worked on the former London Underground electric trains twixt Ryde and Shanklin. His sudden death was obviously a great loss to wife, family and workmates, but happy memories of Frank live on.

Tony Tiltman

Since the publication of *Once Upon A Line Volume One* and reading my reminiscences contained therein, many more memories have come flooding back, like the day we ran through gates with the Ventnor goods at Blackwater in 1946. As we rounded the curve from Shide the distant signal indicated that the line ahead was clear. At

Above: **Former Fireman Frank Ash pictured on No. 36 *Caris-brooke* at Newport shed following a day's work on the Ventnor West push-pull service.** June Ash Collection.

Below: **Driver Frank Ash prepares to set off to work from his home at Blackwater station.** *June Ash Collection.*

Below: **Left, Andrew Britton and right, Driver Ken West pictured outside Ryde St John's Road shed after a footplate ride on No. 24 *Calbourne*.**

John A. Britton

Two footplate friends at work, Driver Ted Dale takes water for his thirsty engine, No. 32 *Bonchurch*, while Fireman Frank Ash enjoys a break from the shovel back on the footplate.

June Ash Collection.

the approach to the station Driver Harry Watson noticed that the crossing gates were closed. Immediately the brakes were applied full on and the whistle was sounded. When we eventually came to a halt the guard's van at the rear of the sixty wagon train was on the crossing. The guard, poor old Bill Symes scrambled out with cuts and bruises and luckily there was no serious damage to our E1 tank locomotive. At the official inquiry it was discovered that the signal wire had expanded during the previous day and overnight the wire had contracted to pull the signal off position. My driver, Harry 'Toby' Watson and I had a very lucky escape that morning.

I had always been told as a boy that railways were very dangerous and that I always had to wait until the train stopped before climbing down. This lesson was dramatically brought home to me one night at Cowes, shortly after becoming a fireman. Cowes station was on a slight gradient positioned on a curve. After drawing to a halt my driver, 'Rubbles' Coleman and I, prepared the engine, No. 31 *Chale* to run around our train. As we waited to carry out this operation, our guard drew our attention to something going on at the rear of the train. We walked along the platform to discover to our horror that a passenger had jumped off the train before

it had stopped. In so doing the poor chap had slipped down and been cut in half by the carriage wheels. This is a terrible incident to recall, but if someone reading this learns from the tale then it would have been well worth telling.

My regular engine as a fireman working from Newport depot was engine No. 34 *Newport* and her driver was Tom Hayward. I stayed with No. 34 for about six years. She was a super engine – very free steaming. Our opposite turn crew was Dick Hollands and Fred Janaway. My next engine was No. 25 *Godshill* and her driver was Jim Stone. I got on well with both my regular drivers but not everyone could get on with Driver Hayward who was a London 'cockney' and liked everything "ship shape and Bristol fashion". If ever I was required to do a driving turn when working with Tom Hayward my replacement fireman would sometimes take a day off work sick rather than 'put up' with poor Tom. When I transferred to Ryde shed as a driver, I took over from O.P. 'Rabbits' Vallender who was a driver on No. 24 *Calbourne*. My opposite turn driver to begin with was Bill Miller and later with Ken West when Bill retired. My regular fireman was John Farrington. I had hardly any trouble with No. 24, with the exception of tubes blowing. "If they have as good a time with 24 *Calbourne* in preservation as I did with BR, they won't go far wrong."

Footnote: According to Harry Watson the engine involved in the Blackwater crossing incident was No. 1 *Medina* with 14 wagons and one coach plus a brake van in the summer of 1946.

Above: **With a full head of steam, No. 24 Calbourne restarts the 09.18 to Cowes away from Haven Street on 4th October 1965. The cameraman is carefully observed by Fireman John Farrington who can be seen peering from 24's cab.**

John Goss

Opposite page top: **Driver Tony Tiltman opens up the regulator of No. 28 *Ashey*, making a lively start from Cowes, with a train for Ryde on the last day of operation of the Cowes line services in February 1966.**

G. S. Cocks

Right: **Fireman Tony Tiltman prepares to collect the single line token from the Newport North signalman as he heads away from Newport station on No. 32 *Bonchurch* with a train for Cowes.**

A. Tiltman Collection

Right: The young fireman, Tony Tiltman, pictured aboard "Terrier" tank No. 8 *Freshwater* at Ventnor West station in 1945, but where is the driver? He is sitting at the other end of the train in the driving coach operating the controls of the push-pull unit, leaving poor Tony to do all the hard work back on the engine!
A. Tiltman Collection

Below: Driver Tom Hayward stands beside his regular engine, No. 34 *Newport* while his fireman Tony Tiltman poses for the cameraman on the footplate, prior to moving off Newport shed to haul a service train to Freshwater.
A. Tiltman Collection

Arthur Wiltshire

The Isle of Wight railways were a good stepping stone in my railway career, for I started work originally for the London & South Western Railway as a cleaner at Eastleigh shed, near Southampton in 1917. Soon after the grouping in to the 'Big Four' railway companies I was able to get promotion as a fireman at Newport shed in 1924.

My first impressions of Isle of Wight railway staff were not favourable. I remember arriving at Cowes off a Red Funnel paddle steamer and pushing my possessions up to Cowes station. As I was about to board the Newport bound train, hauled by a Beyer, Peacock 2-4-0 tank engine the Station Master approached me. I introduced myself as a new fireman bound for Newport shed, but Mr Otto Hill the Station Master was only interested in my extra luggage. I informed him that I was transporting

Above: **Repairs are in hand at Blackwater Gates in the summer of 1946, following their partial demolition by an E1 tank engine driven by Harry 'Toby' Watson and fired by Tony Tiltman. Pictured at work are, left to right, Labourer Fred Bartrum, Sub-ganger Harry Lowe, Labourer Frank Porter and Carpenter William Jolliffe.**

J. R. G. Griffiths

Below: **Problems galore with both sets of gates at Blackwater! Flagman Roy Hale (left), Labourer Fred Bartrum and Sub-ganger Harry Lowe assist Carpenter William Jolliffe with repair work.**

J. R. G. Griffiths

"Rubbles" Coleman, a real terror when it came to crossing gates that were not open for him to proceed on his way.

a small Brighton 0-6-0 "Terrier" tank, No. 11 *Newport*. Our opposite turn driver was Wilf Smart and he warned me to keep the old girl, No. 11, in first class condition . . . or else! In those days we worked her out on the Ventnor West push-pull link and occasionally up to Freshwater. Each Saturday night about 8 pm we would work down into Sandown with the push-pull set and then full regulator back to Newport. Number 11 was a lovely little engine until one day she went into works for a general overhaul. Three days after she returned we had her out on the Ventnor West push-pull service and we were gently easing her in. At Ventnor West a metallic packed gland blew and when we came to examine the damage we noted that the plate had buckled. An urgent message went out to send for Ken Meaning the mechanical wizard of Newport shed. He duly arrived and confirmed that what we had suspected was correct. He pointed out that the works staff should have put in asbestos packing. Anyway Ken told us to give her a run up to St Lawrence tunnel which was the summit of the Ventnor West branch and then coast down to Merstone. The run back to Merstone was stop and start every $\frac{1}{4}$

an old sewing machine to my new digs. He then asked me to purchase an extra ticket for this excess baggage! What a way to treat your fellow railwaymen I thought.

I soon made friends with other lads in a similar position to me, who had come over to the Island, such as Ted Joyce who made me feel particularly at home and kept my spirits high. I was soon introduced to my first regular driver, Ernie Chiverton and our regular engine,

"Terrier" tank locomotive No. 11 *Newport* pictured at Ventnor West in 1924 with Driver Frank Chiverton and Guard Bert Pullinger standing at rail level, while Fireman Arthur Wiltshire looks on from the footplate. Today this little Brighton "Terrier" tank survives in active retirement at the Isle of Wight Steam Railway, Haven Street, where she is maintained and driven by Len Pullinger, who is the nephew of the guard pictured here.

Arthur Wiltshire Collection

mile with steam blowing out all over the place, but as Ken predicted we made it back to Merstone where she was towed away by an O2 tank.

My next driver was Alf Ainsworth and our regular engine was the Drummond boilered O2 tank No. 29 *Alverstone*. She was a strong free-steaming engine almost like a Drummond M7 in appearance. To my mind the Drummond boilered O2 tanks were far stronger than the Adams boilered engines. For speed also they were superb as we proved on a special trial run down from Ventnor. If I remember correctly we reached over 60 mph – not bad considering we were usually confined to a maximum of 40 mph.

At the outbreak of war I was amused to see that the wagons and carriages on the Ventnor West branch were shunted into St Lawrence tunnel each night. This only lasted for a short time that I remember. Not long after

Above: **Ready for the run down to Ventnor West. Pictured here at Merstone aboard their regular engine, No. 11 *Newport* are Arthur Wiltshire (left) and Driver Alf Ainsworth.**
Arthur Wiltshire Collection

Above: **Fireman Arthur Wiltshire pictured here aboard No. 11 *Newport* shortly after arrival at Ventnor West.**
Arthur Wiltshire Collection

Left: **A picture taken from the inside carriage of a Ventnor West push-pull carriage set mid-way between Whitwell and Godshill. Peering out from the cab of the engine is Fireman Arthur Wiltshire, while Driver Alf Ainsworth looks on through the cab spectacle.**
Arthur Wiltshire Collection

Left: **Having just arrived from Freshwater and Yarmouth the train crew and inspector pose for the camera in front of engine No. 30 *Shorwell* at Freshwater Bay platform in Newport station. Left to right are Fireman Arthur Wiltshire, Eastleigh Locomotive Inspector, Guard Charles Matthews and Driver Alf Ainsworth.**

Arthur Wiltshire Collection

Below: **Rogues' Gallery! Left to right, Driver Alf Ainsworth, Guard, Bert Pullinger and Fireman Arthur Wiltshire take a rest in between duties at Newport station.**

Arthur Wiltshire Collection

in mid-1940, I was promoted to be a driver at Salisbury on the West of England expresses to Exeter. As I roared along the lines on 'Merchant Navy' ("Packet") Pacifics, I often remembered the small engines and my pals on the Isle of Wight.

Ron Read

Like so many before me my story began at Ryde locomotive shed starting off as a cleaner. In May 1937, I joined Eddie Prangnell, Mike Tucker, Roy Rodwell and other

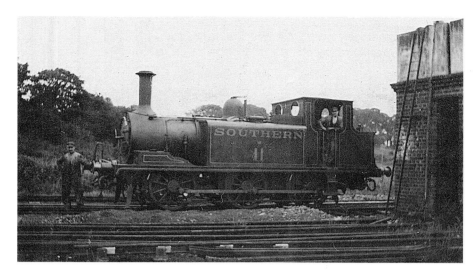

"Terrier" tank No. 11 *Newport*. Standing by the front buffer beam is Driver Alf Ainsworth and in the cab Fireman Arthur Wiltshire.

Arthur Wiltshire Collection

Engine No. 11 *Newport* prepares to return to its carriage stock following a spell of shunting at Freshwater.

Arthur Wiltshire Collection

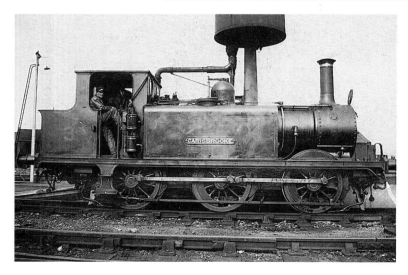

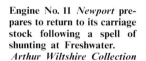

With their regular engine in shed for boiler washout, Fireman Arthur Wiltshire and Driver Alf Ainsworth are given the spare engine, No. 3 *Carisbrooke* for the day. They are pictured waiting in Freshwater Bay platform at Newport on 4th June 1930.

Arthur Wiltshire Collection

21

notable enginemen on that first rung of the ladder to be an engine driver. The Charge Hand at the time was Chad Willis and he explained to us boy cleaners that locomotives were always divided into four parts for our purposes: the underneath – the motion, one side of the wheels and frames (twice), the boiler and smokebox.

At Ryde St John's Road shed there would be three or four engines to clean on our shift. Somehow the Newport based locomotives could never come up to the Ryde standard of cleaning – Chad Willis would always make sure of that. His policy was to carefully check thoroughly around each engine with a light flare and ensure the cleaning was done to the highest standard, although he had only one eye! Discipline was strict and Chad would never allow cleaners to have more than their allotted thirty minute break, although some nights he would drop off to sleep. During such periods we would all gather together with a pack of playing cards and climb up in between the motion of our last engine. By carefully placing a piece of wood on the motion we had a table top. The game went well until Chaddy woke up. He would sneak up onto the footplate, blow the locomotive's whistle and shout out the number of the engine and make out to move it. The 'card school' would scramble down through the motion with cards, table top and money cascading down everywhere.

From the summer of 1938, I was given the opportunity to go out on occasional firing turns. My wage for cleaning was 4s 11d (25p) per day but this figure increased to 9s 6d (47½p) when firing. Once a cleaner had got 313 firing duties under his belt, he was entitled to the full 9s 6d regardless. In those early days of the Second World War this feat seemed impossible, but I was able to gain some valuable experience firing to drivers like Bill Miller, Fred Cass, Bill Vallender and Jack Bradford. Each driver had his own particular customs and techniques for driving and each engine had its own peculiarities.

On one firing turn they sent me out on No. 22 *Brading* with Driver 'Mad' Jack Sturgess, with a semi-fast from Ryde Pier Head to Ventnor. We went like the "Flying Scotsman" as far as Sandown where Jack asked me to collect the token. This was fine but at Shanklin the token exchange went a little wrong.

Just as I was about to exchange, the signalman noticing that it was engine 22, ie 'Mad' Jack's locomotive, decided to move back a fraction. This caused me to miss it, and the token hit the back of my hand over the knuckles and bounced up the platform just missing passengers. Jack immediately slammed on the Westinghouse brakes for me to run back and collect it. We had a full load on behind and a couple of box vans for good measure, therefore the climb out of Shanklin up Apse Bank from a dead stop was quite demanding for our O2 tank. We slipped a little, but 'Mad' Jack kept her steady and with a lot of barking from our Drummond chimney we made it to the top of the bank.

On another occasion, when Jack's engine *Brading* must have been in for boiler washout, we were given a little Brighton "Terrier" tank No. 11 *Newport* which is now preserved on the Isle of Wight Steam Railway. We first had a run up to Medina Wharf, where we collected a wagon train of gas coal for Sandown, Shanklin and Ventnor. A Newport guard named George Brown greeted us, complete with usual red carnation in the buttonhole of his uniform. With a green light from George, Jack opened *Newport's* regulator and once we got some momentum going we began to pick up speed. We had a clear-road through Newport, Shide, Blackwater, Merstone and so on. However, as we passed through Alverstone she began to slow down and the weight of the heavy coal wagons began to tell on the little Brighton tank. At last she drew to a halt on the bank up to Sandown, which curved with a check rail. Without warning she slipped and Jack dropped sand down on to the rails to give the wheels greater adhesion, but she continued to "lose her feet" and my fire was just going up the chimney. Our losing battle in the darkness must have woken the whole of Sandown up and provided them with a free firework display with the red hot ash from the

Driver Ted 'Bogie' Willis on the platform and Fireman Ron Read on the footplate of No. 21 *Sandown*, ready for departure to Ryde Pier Head.
Peter Joyce Collection

Polished to perfection, complete with Caledonian style star on the smokebox door, No. 3 *Ryde* waits at her namesake shed at Ryde St John's Road.

Peter Joyce Collection

chimney. Jack asked me to go back and see the guard, but he was already on his way up to see us on the engine. I left the driver and guard to work things out on the footplate of No. 11, while I ran up the line to see the signalman at Sandown.

Luckily, the Sandown signalman had already guessed what had happened and authorised George and Jack to halve the train. George uncoupled the train into two equal portions, allowing Jack to proceed up the gradient in Sandown. This left poor George with the second half which we anticipated returning to collect within minutes. It was a great idea, but little did we realise after leaving our friendly guard that he would be running back to Alverstone chasing his half of the train. Apparently, when we reversed to 'close up' for George to uncouple we must have hit up a little hard. Only the brake in George's guard's van had been screwed down, and in the heat of the moment he had forgotten to apply the brakes on some of his wagons. When we returned light engine on our "Terrier" to collect the second half of the train, we were amazed to find it had gone and even more surprised how far it had travelled in such a short time.

For a period of time, I went out firing on No. 15 *Cowes* to Driver Fred Cass. She was usually a good steamer and a joy to fire. One morning we were asked to have a new driver with us to 'learn the road' for a couple of days – his name was Arnold Nye and he was fresh from the Army. Upon arrival at Ventnor with a train from Ryde, we uncoupled our O2 tank and ran around the carriages, after taking water as usual. With everything ready for the return journey, Driver Cass invited the new driver and me across to the pub for some liquid refreshment. Arnold refused preferring to stay on the engine. On returning from the pub, I opened the fire-box doors and to my astonishment and horror observed that the fire was almost out!

Whatever had our visiting driver been doing with himself I wondered? Nevertheless, putting all thoughts of what had or had not been done out my mind, I set to work on getting some sort of fire going. The guard's whistle blew and we were off. Coming out of Ventnor through the tunnel it was one hell of a slow crawl, and we somehow limped into Wroxall. Meanwhile, Fred had done the gentlemanly thing by taking his hat off and hanging it over the brass steam pressure gauge – only daring to take it off between Smallbrook and Ryde St Johns. Needless to say there was more hot air in the cab than in the fire, resulting in Driver Arnold Nye never venturing to ride with us again.

Dan J. Wheeler

My railway career on the Island did not begin in the usual engine driver pattern of cleaner, fireman, then driver, but commenced at the outbreak of the Second World War in the Traffic Department. My first recollections are as a Junior Porter at Horringford station on the Newport-Merstone-Sandown line.

It was a delightfully rural station as this incident will

illustrate. A passenger train arrived from Newport with Charlie Matthews as its guard, a very smartly turned out railwayman with brushed hat and uniform and polished shiny black boots. Attached to the rear of his train were a collection of cattle trucks containing one hundred sheep. Fences were prepared to act as a barrier across the platform to drive the sheep into the blocked sidings. Charlie hailed to me, "Whoosh them out", but I was a country lad and only 4 ft 10 in high so the big kind Guard Matthews decided to lend a hand. You can imagine what he looked like in that Southern Railway uniform after – I couldn't stop laughing.

A few weeks later on using the gent's toilet I became locked in as the lock was faulty. I yelled for at least an hour for Mrs Callaway living in the Station House to rescue me, but I was only heard at 'Stickworth Hall' and they didn't trouble themselves. Presently a train arrived from Newport and whistled for the distant and home signals to be pulled off to allow the train to continue its journey to Sandown. The next thing I heard was the fireman from the locomotive tramping along the platform who of course duly released me. However, after this little incident I had a lot of leg-pull and was known as the boy who got locked in the loo. The next day my opposite number, Syd Dennett suffered the same fate but he was able to knock out a panel from the door with the cistern lid. Eventually, Jimmy James came along to repair the lock and the remains of the door.

From 1940, I moved along the line to Newchurch. Here wooden flower boxes were sent in threes to Covent Garden in London, each set weighing approximately 30 lb. As luck would have it my favourite guard, Charlie Matthews would be the guard on the train they were sent on. Charlie's technique was to stack these flower boxes up to 6 ft high, until one day he called out as usual, "Whoosh them in boy" and one landed on Charlie's size twelve boots. You should have seen poor Charlie dancing around the guard's compartment of the brake coach. I laughed and laughed until he clipped my ear!

In 1942, 'Mr Hitler' interrupted my railway service and I joined the Royal Marines until 1946. On return in August 1946, I worked at Wootton and Ashey stations on the Ryde–Newport–Cowes line. At Ashey, I recall a train arriving from Ryde with guard Den Squibb freshly demobbed from the Air Force. Inside the brake van was a box of clucking hens bound for Newport. "Would you like a couple of eggs for breakfast?" asked the guard. On replying yes, he promptly began the guts out of the crate until the hens produced the right number of eggs, much to my amazement!

Two days later the same train with same guard pulled into Ashey station. This time Den had boxes of plums for Newport. As usual he alighted from his train to ensure everyone was aboard and the doors were locked. With a mouth full of plum, flag in right hand, plum in left which he endeavoured to throw to me, the train moved off towards Haven Street, minus its guard. The last I saw of him was this nimble figure running down the track to catch his train – I suppose he did.

In September 1946, I transferred to the Locomotive Department at Ryde St John's Road. From 1947, I was

out on the road firing to Driver O.P. 'Rabbits' Vallender on the Brading–Bembridge branch. One day we were heading bunker first aboard an O2 tank and as we approached the Cement Crossing a bullock came into view standing on the line. It was too late to stop and we hit it full in the backside with the right hand side buffer. Somehow this bullock managed to clear the fence in one leap without leaving anything behind. He disappeared at about 90 mph across the marsh.

A year passed and the Island railways were adjusting to Nationalisation. My memory of this period focuses on a journey on the Ventnor–Ryde Pier Head line with Driver Sid Craig. We were heading down Apse Bank with six coaches behind, fully loaded with passengers for the Ryde–Portsmouth paddle steamer. Sid Craig was about five foot high and as we were heading bunker first towards Ryde his custom was to stand on a piece of sleeper, otherwise he would be unable to view the line ahead through the spectacle window of the bunker. At the end of the straight section of line from Three Arch bridge approaching Shanklin, there is a crossing. I spotted a tractor and trailer loaded with ex-'D' Day 'Pluto' pipes straddling the track. There must have been about fifty in number, approximately thirty feet in length – almost as high as the top of our locomotive bunker. Immediately, I gave warning to Sid who fell off his sleeper end. While I applied the brake, Sid somehow managed to throw the locomotive's reversing lever into full reverse. We both ended up bent double under the bunker.

The front of the locomotive bunker struck this lot causing little damage and we pulled up roughly two coach lengths along. The pipes meanwhile went like matchsticks and the tractor's driver ended up in the blackberries and was only badly shocked, but the faces of the passengers peering from the carriage stock told the story of our narrow escape.

The following summer of 1949, I was sent out with Driver Alf Goodson to fire on the infamous No. 22 *Brading*. This engine seemed to bring out motivation for tricks with its footplate crews – I was no exception! One particular Sunday my attention turned to a family enjoying a picnic in their garden, in the first bungalow past the second bridge out of Shanklin. As we blasted our way up Apse Bank under the bridge, I slipped a couple of good shovels into *Brading's* firebox ensuring they spread across the fire and shut the door fast. "That did the trick!" They couldn't see across their garden for red hot ash and smoke. On the return journey from Ventnor to Ryde, I didn't feel so smug as the Fire Brigade had been called and the family had lost their garden shed.

A few weeks later on *Brading*, we arrived at Ryde Pier Head station in platform 2. We pushed back the train to unhook and run-round. Waiting at the end of the station on the buffer blocks for the dummy ground signal to indicate the points were set for us to run around, No. 22 decided to make its own shunt. First the engine hit the blocks then rebounded onto the carriage stock. This happened three times. Somehow we wrestled with the controls, but the Westinghouse brake leaked off leav-

Fireman Dan Wheeler opens wide the regulator of No. 16 *Ventnor* as he sets off from Ryde Esplanade in 1950. Meanwhile, Driver Nelson Parsons take a turn at the shovel.

Reg Harris

ing no handbrake on the locomotive. The passengers gasped in amazement.

At times drivers were sent over to the Isle of Wight to help with the summer time-table crisis period, when all hands on deck were required. In the summer of 1949 Driver Reg Harris was sent over from Basingstoke on loan. On such occasions the fireman's knowledge of the Island lines was invaluable. One evening, the Basingstoke driver and I were sent out to work the late freight from St Helens to Sandown with Dick Randell as our guard. The thirty wagon length freight was halted at Brading home signal, to shunt out a wagon of coal. We eased up and Reg unhooked. Little did we know that our

guard Dick Randell had meanwhile dropped off into the land of dreams in his brake van. As soon as Reg had unhooked, the wagons decided to make their own way back to St Helens. Now Reg decided to chase after his runaway train attempting to pin down as many wagon brakes as possible. With the Basingstoke driver running and falling over in his attempts to pin down the wagon brakes and me papping the whistle on the following engine we must have made an amusing sight to the farming community alongside the line.

At last Dick woke up but couldn't make things out, except that he was going the wrong way. In the end he had sense enough to stop the runaway before the whole

Fireman Dan Wheeler picking up colleague Reg Harris at his lodgings in 1949

Dan Wheeler

25

A regular engine on the Bembridge branch for many years, No. 15 *Cowes*. This front end picture of an O2 tank shows off well detail for modellers such as the Westinghouse brake pump, Drummond chimney, smokebox door and riveting. Could the clean appearance be due to the handywork of Dan Wheeler?

J. R. G. Griffiths

26

lot ended up in the sea at St Helen's Quay. Suffice to say, we set off back to Brading for another go hoping that the shield of darkness would hide our red faces.

From 1950 to 1954 I mostly had the good fortune to fire with Driver Nelson Parsons. The work was hard, but with Nelson at the regulator it was fun and one could learn a tremendous amount from his vast experience. He was a real character as this anecdote will illustrate. It was a blistering hot summer Saturday at Ryde Pier Head station, and after squaring up the fire in preparation for our journey to Ventnor we discovered we had fifteen minutes to spare. As luck would have it the tide was high and the calm blue sea looked so inviting, so Nelson suggested we strip off and dive into the sea to cool off and kill the time. Once in the water time passed all too quickly and you can imagine the panic when the guard blew his whistle and we were still in the sea under the pier. We clambered back up on to the footplate and endeavoured to dry ourselves with sponge cloths. With the regulator wide open, the little O2 tank set off down the pier towards the Esplanade station with the two of us struggling to climb back into our overalls.

Working the night Ventnor–Ryde freight I began to appreciate that Driver Parsons only drove at one speed – 'flat out'. As the gradient was mostly down hill to Shanklin, and with a good head of steam I sat back in the fireman's seat. As we approached Wroxall home signal, Nelson tried to apply the brake ready for the staff exchange, as he thought it was a fitted freight which would have had more braking power. On this occasion it was not so as the wagons were all loose coupled. The Wroxall porter–signalman, Harold Unstead appeared on the platform ready to exchange the single line staff and we swept through the station and accelerated down the bank towards Shanklin. Upon arrival at Shanklin signalman Reg Smith stared in disbelief. Signalman Unstead had rung through and said "don't expect them to stop as they have just passed me at 60 mph plus!". He added that he had spun round three times and found the staff in his hand!

Firing steam locomotives is not all glamour and romance. Drivers and firemen sweat buckets in the course of a journey and need to replenish lost body liquid. Thus at the end of a particularly hectic journey from Ventnor, Nelson offered me a pint of the best bitter at "The First and Last" at Ryde Pier Head. After attending to the locomotive's requirements we set off up platform 4 to attend to the crew's requirements. As we sat down to appreciate our gold coloured nectar, I had a horrible feeling that someone was on our engine, so I quickly downed the remainder of my drink. Saying nothing to Nelson, I ran down the whole length of the cat walk behind the train to just beat a keen Locomotive Inspector coming onto the engine footplate, from the platform side. "Good afternoon, fireman. I thought I had a catch!" exclaimed the stern voice. Nelson never could understand how I knew something was wrong – but just put it down to a fireman's sixth sense.

Railways run in my family as Des Gallop my brother-in-law was also a fireman. Often he would tell me about his experiences and he related one amusing incident to

me whilst firing to Driver Jim Hunnybun on No. 14 *Fishbourne*, aboard the first passenger train of the morning from Ventnor. Approaching Wroxall Jim applied the Westinghouse air brake ready to stop in the platform, but nothing happened. Instead the train continued through Wroxall station out to Three Arch bridge, before Jim could negotiate climbing along the framing to the first coach, in order to open the taps to create a passage for the air brakes in the train. The train then stopped and reversed back to Wroxall for passengers to alight and the exchange of the staff.

Sadly in 1954 I had to leave my friends on the Island for promotion as a driver at a mainland depot, but these years will remain in my memory as the happiest of my life.

Did You Know?
by Peter Henry
(Reproduced by permission of D.J. Wheeler)

The railway line from Ventnor West
Now has ceased to function
A similar thing will take place soon
On Brading Bembridge junction.

The reason for this prophecy
A story I will tell
Of a driver and a fireman
On the Brading Bembridge Belle.

One Tuesday evening after ten
At the St Helen's stop
I along with my two brothers
And another pal called Bop.

Were hailed from a cab engine by
A fellow bathed in sweat
You lucky fellows bin drinking
And I ain't finished work yet.

I was puzzled by this statement
As the train gathered speed
There on the back were three coaches
For which there was not a need.

Searching in vain for passengers
The last coach came in line
Three voices spoke in unison
That Danny was wasting time.

You see the reason for saying
The line will soon shut down
Poor Danny will have to retire
In his birthplace Brading Town.

Ron Connor

I have the Isle of Wight railways to thank for so much, for it was my good friend and fellow fireman Andy Ross that introduced me to my wife (his cousin) whilst on holiday at Edinburgh. In fact, a job on the railways was not a first choice career to begin with, and it was only meant to be a temporary job at the outset.

Once I started as a cleaner at Newport shed, I found that I liked the job. Eventually I was to become regular fireman to Driver Walter Gear on engine No. 31 *Chale*. Although as a 'passed man' during the summer season I was often called upon to drive engines. At Newport shed everyone was so warm and friendly, even the boiler washer Mr Toogood made wooden boxes for us to keep our sandwiches and books in.

When I began cleaning at Newport back in 1944, we used to have to work night shifts. Once the locomotives were clean however we could go back to our cabin for a sleep. On one occasion the fitters complained to the charge hand about our work and we had to go back out and clean the engines again from start to finish. We all thought of different schemes to get our own back on the fitters who were by now asleep in a disused railway carriage body provided for them. Now the fitters had boarded up most of the windows and sealed all but one of the doors. This we saw as an Achilles heel and we set about on a devious plan to even the score. One cleaner acquired some detonators from an engine, climbed up onto the roof of the carriage and promptly dropped the detonators down the chimney on to their stove. We then all dispersed onto various locomotives and set about our work. Presently there was a loud explosion causing the whole stove to disintegrate. Hot coke and coal flew onto the slumbering fitters and the chimney pipe collapsed showering them with black soot. There was hell to play, but they couldn't prove anything as we were all busy at work.

Cleaners at Newport were always getting up to tricks with new cleaners. The new boy was, often as not, sent to get the cleaning rags up in the corner of the sand bin. The young innocent lad would climb up the ladder and into the sand which was often almost red hot. This sand was of course used by drivers in the locomotive sand-boxes. How these lads escaped serious injury I'll never know. Alternatively another fool's errand for the new boy was to send him into the firebox of a locomotive that had only hours before dropped its fire. Equipped with a small hand brush he was instructed to sweep the brick arch. Once inside the firebox the young cleaner's overalls would begin to smoulder and he would sweat like someone in a Turkish bath. If one wanted to be really nasty they would close the Adam's O2's firebox doors and light a piece of oily rag underneath. It's a wonder somebody was never killed.

One morning there was a hair raising incident with a cleaner who had dropped off to sleep on the motion of one of the O2 tanks. The driver discovered him whilst he was oiling round, but if he had moved the locomotive before discovering the cleaner he would without doubt have been killed.

Whilst on day shift cleaning duties I was able to witness a unique occurrence at Newport shed; when boiler washer Jarvis did some running repairs to an O2 whilst she was still in full steam. The engine came in to the shed following a run from Freshwater and the driver drew our attention to a leaking washout plug in the smokebox. Rather than fail the engine and drop the fire to remedy the problems, Mr Jarvis climbed into the smokebox, equipped with a special long thin wire tool. He then proceeded to tighten up the tapes and plug whilst the steam whisped around him, mixed with sulphurous fumes from the fire. It was a dangerous touch and go repair for if the plug had become dislodged he would have been scalded with boiling steam resulting in certain death. Such was the enthusiasm to keep all engines at Newport in full working order.

Later on in my footplate career, I had two other experiences illustrating just how dangerous railway work can be. The first incident happened one night in pitch darkness at Newport shed. We came in to the shed with No. 31 *Chale,* and after halting in front of the shed I cleaned out the firebox. My driver, Walter Gear then asked me to hold tight while he moved forward with *Chale* over the inspection pits, in order for him to be more accessible to oil the motion under the engine. After completing my work in the smokebox I stepped off the buffer beam down on to the ground level, as I thought. Not so, I had forgotten the locomotive had moved forwards and I descended down into the pit. In so doing, I knocked myself out.

The next encounter I had with a dangerous situation was while working on the Ventnor West branch. We arrived at Merstone with a Brighton "Terrier", which I believe was No. 8 *Freshwater,* only to discover that we were unable to pull off the main Sandown–Newport line into the refuge siding. Signalman Syd Dennett then gave us permission to reverse back up to the Ventnor West branch approach line. Driver Gear gave me permission as a passed man to drive the engine back. Having secured the engine and screwed down the handbrake, I proceeded to walk back along the track to join Walt Gear in the signal box for a cup of tea with Syd Dennett. As I whistled my way along the track I forgot that the Ventnor West line joined the line coming in from Sandown. Presently, I heard several loud shreaks of a whistle and as I turned to my horror I saw the approaching train from Sandown. I do hope that those who read of my experiences, and who work on preserved lines, will learn to respect just how dangerous railways can be when one is not fully alert.

One of the most underestimated types of engines that worked on the Island were the former London, Brighton & South Coast Railway E1 class tanks. I had some luck with this class of Island locomotive as Driver Arthur Turner stepped in to help me when I was getting rather short of steam one day on No. 2 *Yarmouth.* His technique was to fire through the half moon flap and sprinkle the coal over the top. The firebox grate sloped towards the front end and the secret was to keep the fire as flat as possible as you looked at it, but in practice the side profile would be a wedge shape. With a good fire and consequently a good head of steam, the E1 engines would easily walk away with forty wagons up Fairlee Bank leading out of Newport. Likewise the E1 tanks had a great pulling capacity when on passenger trains. They would easily maintain timings on the "Tourist" through Ventnor–Newport–Freshwater train.

SOUTHERN RAILWAY

(4/47)

Stock.
(1269/4-37.)

PILOTMAN'S TICKET.

To be used when it is necessary to work the traffic of a single line by Pilotman owing to failure of the Electric Tablet, Staff or Key-token Apparatus, or when the Electric Tablet, Staff or Key-token or Train Staff has been lost or is defective.

SPECIMEN

To the GUARD and DRIVER of _____ Train.

From _____ To _____

You are authorised to proceed from _____

to _____ Pilotman following.

Signature of Pilotman _____

Date _____

[See Over

The only reason Ryde men did not like them was because they were not totally familiar with them. It is a pity that an E1 is not preserved at Haven Street to join the other two types of Island classes represented for use on the Isle of Wight Steam Railway.

I did have a very amusing half hour's work on an E1 engine, which I think was No. 4 *Wroxall*. We had hauled a forty wagon coal train from Medina Wharf to Newport Yard. After pulling into the 'up' loop platform line on the locomotive shed side of the station, my driver, Toby Watson was greeted by Station Foreman Jack Fish. He asked us to 'fly-shunt' three wagons into number five siding for dispatch to Wootton, five in to number four siding for Brading, twelve in to number three siding for Sandown and Ventnor etc. Now the principle of 'fly-shunting' is to propel the wagons, the shunter uncouples, the locomotive and remaining wagon halt leaving the loose wagons to continue along the siding on their own. Now on this occasion Driver Watson was not pulling up quick enough and Foreman Fish was unable to uncouple properly. Eventually the ginger-headed Station Foreman walked up to the engine and told the driver to give the wagons a good push and pull up hard of the points. Driver Toby Watson duly followed his instructions and opened the regulator of *Wroxall*, 'wide open'

Below: **A superb front end view of E1 class engine No. 4 *Wroxall* waiting patiently at Smallbrook Junction with a coal train from Medina Wharf. Signalman Vic Hailes recalls that the fireman on the locomotive was none other than Fireman Ron Connor, and his driver on this occasion was Jack Sewell.**

J. R. G. Griffiths

and when the signal was given by Foreman Fish to stop, Driver Watson applied the brake fully and threw the reversing lever right back into full reverse. This resulted in a coupling snapping with the chain literally flying up into the air. Several ex-Brighton open plank wagons, fully loaded with coal, shot off at top speed to the end of the siding resulting in two going completely over the end buffer stop blocks. All I could see from the footplate of the E1 tank was a black cloud of coal dust completely covering the area from the signal box, across the sidings to the engine shed – as if a bomb had gone off. Foreman Jack Fish's face just looked in disbelief, but his instructions had been followed to the letter.

Mention of Brighton locomotives on the Isle of Wight, brings to mind my work with E4 class 0-6-2T tank No. 2510. She came to the Island in 1946 as an answer to the need for a more powerful type of engine to work the Ryde to Ventnor trains. The idea was to use this locomotive on push and pull trains. Before being imported to the Island via Medina Wharf, she had received extensive modifications at Eastleigh Works to adapt her to the Island loading gauges, which included shortening the chimney. To begin with she was sent from Medina Wharf where she was unloaded and sent to Ryde shed. Here they discovered that on trials the E4's clearances were too tight for various platforms, owing to the long coupled wheelbase. This locomotive was then banned from working between Ryde and Ventnor. They also said that the E4's coal consumption was poor in

comparison with the O2 class. As a consequence No. 2510 was sent to us at Newport, where she became the spare engine. The men at Newport by comparison got on well with this engine and she worked again between Ventnor, Wroxall, Shanklin, Sandown, Merstone and Newport on the "Tourist" through train. I personally ran on this service firing No. 2510 on a number of occasions. We experienced no problems and she ran at speed non-stop between Sandown and Merstone.

The footplate of the E4, was very roomy with plenty of space for us to walk around. She had a piano-top style back which gave us a feeling of luxury. Contrary to popular belief, its brakes worked well for those who knew how to use them. On the Freshwater line, she worked well but was over-powered. It would have been better if they had sent over a "Teddy Bear" Ivatt 2-6-2 tank engine. I feel they would have been ideal for the Island. In 1947, while we still had the E4, there was a terrible winter. I recall going up the Freshwater line and seeing the snow drifts up to the second step, as we passed through Watchingwell.

A few years ago the Daily Telegraph newspaper carried a short article about the way the birds used to follow the trains up Ryde Pier. The reporter, Maurice Burden, assumed that the reason the birds followed the steam

E1 tank No. 4 *Wroxall* pictured outside Newport shed. This engine was a firm favourite with Fireman Connor.

Ronald J. Post

Deep in concentration, Driver Peter Mills takes water at Newport station on 8th June 1964. Meanwhile, back on the footplate, photographer Dick Blenkinsop is accompanied by Inspector Ron Russell who is chatting to Fireman Tony Toogood.

R. J. Blenkinsop

hauled trains was because the steam and smoke from the chimneys of the engines attracted them. This was not exactly correct and I wrote off to the Daily Telegraph and said that the true reason why the birds followed the steam hauled trains was because the gulls were fed crumbs by the footplate crews. It was a game that was played between enginemen and the gulls to see if they could eat the bread crumbs before they dropped down into the water. Even if you threw the crumbs downwards

they would still manage to catch them in time.

During the period when I worked on the Island railways a lot of freight was moved and not just coal either. I recall on one occasion we backed No. 31 *Chale* into the 'down' bay at Newport to collect a 10 ton covered van. From the smell coming from its interior, I deduced that it had just been unloaded with fish. Nobody had bothered to wash it out or put sawdust on the floor. Presently the porters began to load up several boxes of fresh cherries and stacked them box upon box. When they were finished Walt Gear opened *Chale's* regulator and the snatch caused the boxes to topple over resulting in the cherries cascading down on to the van floor. To save time we set about shovelling them up into their wooden box trays, so somewhere someone we hope, enjoyed some "fish flavoured" cherries!

Peter Mills

I hadn't been a fireman long on the Island railways when a very unpleasant accident happened to me on my regular engine, No. 24 *Calbourne*, which is now at Haven Street. In those days coal was in short supply and Ryde shed could only get hold of household coal for the locomotives. I remember being on late turn and squaring up 24's fire, but as we had time to spare I shut the clampers down, closed the firebox doors then climbed down off the footplate to join my driver, Fred Cass. About twenty minutes later I decided to check on *Calbourne's* fire and opened the firebox doors. All I could see was hazy smoke. Then suddenly without warning a sheet of flame exploded, knocking me back across the footplate. The sound of the explosion could be heard inside the shed and Driver Cass came out to investigate. This resulted in me being bandaged up in hospital for several weeks. What had happened was that as soon as I opened the firebox doors oxygen rushed in and thereby ignited various coal gases contained in the household coal. It was a lucky escape and something that I pray will never happen to anyone working on *Calbourne* today at the Isle of Wight Steam Railway.

I first joined the railways in September, 1944 during the later part of the Second World War. As luck would have it I started at Ryde St John's Road shed and never had to move to another depot for promotion. My years on No. 24 as a fireman proved an excellent foundation for my time as a steam driver. When I passed out as a driver, they sent me down to the Brading–Bembridge branch to work the two-coach trains back and forth – believe me it was a monotonous job. We had about thirteen turns on the branch per shift and were given any old engine to work on. By and large it was usually the spare engine from Ryde shed that we had to work on the branch. Following this I gradually worked up to become a driver out on the main line between Ryde and Ventnor. My regular fireman was Tony Toogood, on No. 28 *Ashey* which was a pretty good engine in those days.

Apart from the incident mentioned by Tony Toogood in *Once Upon A Line Volume One,* when I was involved in a shunting derailment at Shanklin, I only had one

Above: **Driver Peter Mills eases engine No. 29** *Alverstone* **over the points and into Ventnor Tunnel after running around the train. Fireman Tony Toogood leans out of the cab to double check the point setting, while up in the signal box the figure of Signalman Harold Fry can be seen pulling the levers, on 31st August 1963.** *G. M. Kichenside*

Below: **Driver Bill Vallender applies No. 16** *Ventnor's* **air brakes as the three-coach train enters Cowes station on 1st June 1958. On the opposite side of the footplate, Fireman Peter Harbour prepares to climb and uncouple when the train has safely stopped.** *G. M. Kichenside*

Left: **Left to right Guard Bert Fallick, Fireman Pete Harbour, Driver Bill Hayward, Fireman John Chambers and on the footplate Driver Bill Vallender.**
Courtesy of Mrs Vallender

other near scrape. Again the locomotive involved was our regular No. 28 *Ashey,* and once more it was on a freight train. We were entering Medina Wharf sidings with a train of empty coal wagons. As we descended down the gradient into the Wharf, the wheels began to slip and the whole locomotive just slid along the rails. Fearing the worst, my fireman, Tony Toogood jumped off the footplate but somehow the train managed to halt on the 'straight road', hitting the buffer blocks.

Peter Harbour and Ron Brett

Peter Harbour

When I started as a cleaner in July, 1945 at Ryde St John's Road shed, I didn't dream for one minute that I would be the driver of the last steam hauled train ever to run on the Isle of Wight in normal service.

Ron Brett

Two years after Pete started work, I joined him at Ryde as a cleaner following my demob from the Army in August 1947 and I finished as a 'passed fireman' mostly driving various O2 tanks. Although our work as cleaners was demanding we still found some time for fun and games. My fellow cleaners and I developed a Ryde shed 'assault-course' which took us lads in and out of the cabin windows, over lockers, down inspection pits and so on. Those same cleaners today have worked their way up, to not only drivers, but one is Depot Supervisor of a major Southern Region locomotive shed!

Peter Harbour

One day one of the cleaners turned up at the shed a changed lad. He had apparently become a converted Christian after listening to an evangelist. The cleaner

Right: **Driver Bill Vallender pictured on the footplate of an O2 tank shortly after transfer from the mainland in 1923. The locomotive is still numbered in her London & South Western Railway identity as 206.**
Courtesy of Mrs Vallender

came in to the shed, stood up on a chair, and began to preach the Gospel and gave a fine sermon to drivers, firemen and cleaners alike. Mid-way through his 'fire and brimstone' speech one of the sinful cleaners acquired the boiler washing hose and turned it on full. The poor lad was washed away off his pulpit and we returned to our 'sinful ways'.

It was not long before I was made up to fireman and my regular driver for the next two years was Harold Nye on No. 19 *Osbourne*. After my period of National Service I returned to Ryde shed to fire No. 17 *Seaview* with Driver Bill Vallender. It was Bill, of course, who was the driver who had his meal delivered ready cooked on a tray whilst working from St John's Road to the Pier and return, each day. On the return trip from Ryde Pier, Bill would always leave some scraps for his dog, and hand over the empty tray to Mrs Vallender making sure she noted the dog's reward. I stayed with Bill on No. 17 for almost ten years and we became really good friends. Towards the end of this period of my service I was sent out on Saturdays to drive on various engines. Following the retirement of Driver Arthur Turner, I was eventually promoted to be driver of No. 25 *Godshill* with Ken Simmonds as my fireman. After 25's withdrawal following her accident at Ryde yard, they gave me No. 28 *Ashey*, and after overhaul she acquired my previous engine's side tanks and flush coupling rods.

Ron Brett

From being a cleaner, my first firing turn was to fire a light engine up the Pier at Ryde. After building up a good head of steam at the shed, Driver Wally Hunnybun informed me that owing to the heavy rain storms Ryde Esplanade Tunnel was flooded. Being green in those days, I listened and acted upon Wally's every word. He suggested to me that I should place some sacks on the floor with lumps of coal on them to prevent them from washing away in the flooded tunnel. As we started away Driver Hunnybun climbed up on to the back boxes of the O2 tank. I thought to myself 'that's a good idea to stop my feet getting wet, I'd better join him'. That was typical of Wally – always up to tricks with new fireman.

My next turn of duty was on the Brading–Bembridge branch on No. 14 *Fishbourne* with Driver Mike Tucker. On the Thursday of my first week with Driver Tucker we changed duties with Driver Jack Bradford and his

A busy scene at Ryde Pier Head on 3rd October 1965, with Fireman Ray Hobden taking water on No. 28 *Ashey* prior to departing with a train for Ventnor. On the right-hand side of the picture, O2 tank No. 26 *Whitwell* backs down on to a train for Newport and Cowes, following its arrival from Ventnor.

G. S. Cocks

fireman. Our new duty was a trip known to Island railwaymen as "round the houses". This involved working from Ryde Pier Head to Sandown, thence to Merstone, Newport and Cowes and finally returning via Newport, Haven Street and Ashey to Ryde – a triangular shaped route. The departure from Sandown was a workmen's train to Cowes and this demanded a good run in order to get the workmen to the ship yards at Cowes on time. Any delay to the schedule meant a loss of pay for the workmen. It was expected that all the stations would be open and gates opened ready for free passage of the train. As our engine left Sandown we could see misty patches towards Alverstone. The visibility conditions worsened at Newchurch as we hit thick fog running alongside the river. Mike slowed down and whistled on the engine's hooter quite frequently, instructing me to keep a sharp eye open for signals. Too late, I spotted a signal which in the fog we assumed was the Horringford distant signal. The next thing I recall was an almighty crash and Driver Tucker applied the brake fully on and put the reversing lever in to full reverse. "We've gone through the gates", I shouted to Mike. We climbed down off the footplate to inspect the damage. Underneath the front driving wheels was the tangled gate and the lamps. Coming down the road around the bend was a milk lorry, which if it had been a few seconds earlier would have no doubt collided with us. After clearing away the debris we discovered that the Westinghouse pipe was damaged. Upon arrival at Newport our engine

was detached for repair but on the return working from Cowes to Ryde, the fitters had completed all necessary repairs. We were therefore able to rejoin our train and continue our turn of duty. Thus I was fully christened into what could happen when things went wrong, but it didn't deter me from firing for Mike for the next two years.

Following my spell on the spare link with Driver Tucker, I joined Driver George Ellis as his regular fireman on No. 30 *Shorwell*. This locomotive was "a pig to fire" owing to the bad condition of its boiler, which was coated with lime scale. No matter how much pressure in the boiler was built up, as soon as the injectors came on, the needle gauge would drop back to a worryingly low reading. It would then prove a devil of a job to regain pressure no matter how good the fire. Now Driver Ellis was a good old time cautious driver, but with the condition of *Shorwell's* boiler to get a good head of steam up Apse Bank required some full regulator. Therefore whenever George turned his back, I would open her up. My driver suspected a loose regulator, but never discovered the true cause. Eventually, the problem was resolved following a general overhaul in Ryde Works.

Peter Harbour

The main talking point each week on the Island railways was how well the railways' football team played. Harry Prangnell from the Parcels Office at Newport

Below left: The trophies awarded to the British Railways Isle of Wight Football Club team 1952-1953. The team were winners of the Isle of Wight League Division Four and Isle of Wight Junior B Cup. They beat Barton Sports 3-2 in the Final, which was played at the old Church Litten Newport Football Club Ground. *The Peter Harbour Collection*

Below right: The British Railways Isle of Wight F.C. team. Pictured left to right are; back row Steve Woods (trainer), Jim Morton (right half), Dennis Snow (Captain, centre half), Ken West (goalkeeper) Dave Williams (left half), Harry Prangnell (Manager). Front row John Duff (left back), Jack Tharme (right back) Bill Firth (outside right), Wilf Riddett (inside right), Jack Miller (centre forward), Derek Cousins (inside left), Harry Hobbs (outside left). Missing from this picture is Peter Harbour who was injured. *The Peter Harbour Collection*

started off the team in the early 1950s, and we began by playing other teams in friendly fixtures. We soon progressed to playing in the Fourth Division of the Island Football League, which we eventually won. In view of the fact that we were all involved in shift work being on the railways, we had a squad to select from nearly two different teams. The sad thing for me was that before the team won the League Cup, I broke my leg in a bad tackle. The results of each match or regular progress reports would be conveyed to those men who were not playing, via passing trains. Hence within minutes of the final whistle they would know in Ventnor and Cowes. It was such a good football team that we won the double – the League and Cup, and when the medals for these competitions were given out we divided them equally between the squad.

Ron Brett

There was a warm friendly atmosphere throughout the Island railway network in those days not just with the football team. One member of Pete's team, Driver Denny Snow used to get up to all sorts of tricks. He once hid a herring fish under the plate of a locomotive's cab, on which we were working. The smell was awful. It wasn't until a couple of weeks later that we discovered it.

Peter Harbour

I remember 'Ginger' Minter tried to get his own back on Driver Snow one day. He waited on the very top of the water column at the Cowes end of Newport station. When Denny Snow pulled in on No. 31 *Chale,* he climbed out of the cab to take water as usual but his eyes somehow caught sight of Driver Minter. Denny then threw a lump of coal at 'Ginger' who ducked to avoid this missile. In so doing however, Driver Minter fell backwards and dropped down into the tank of water. Incidentally this water column tank is now in use at Haven Street. I wonder if they ever get up to similar capers on the preserved railway today?

Another practical joker was Guard Jack Forrester, but one day I managed to turn the joke on Jack. As we approached Newport station platform with a Cowes–Ryde train I spotted the lurking figure of Guard Forrester waiting to dispose of a full bucket of water in my direction. As we approached I caught hold of a large ball of oily waste cotton and aimed it towards the bucket. It landed 'on target' splashing water all over poor Jack.

Ron Brett

One certainly found what a good lot of men worked on the Island railways when things went wrong or difficulties arose. One evening as we were pulling away from Haven Street towards Wootton on No. 30 *Shorwell,* I heard a very strange hissing sound from the outside of our engine. Driver George Ellis braked immediately and we halted before the top of the incline. At first we could not discover the fault, but George spotted that the valve

had come out of the Westinghouse pump. Luckily however, the valve had dropped intact into a pool of oil on the front sandbox. It was therefore, possible for George to make a running repair for us to continue our journey on to Newport.

Peter Harbour

We also experienced a few other difficult problems. I recall running around our set of coaches aboard No. 28 *Ashey* at Ryde Pier. Driver Harold Lacey complained to me that he could hear a strange noise from the exhaust of the chimney. Sure enough when we stopped to investigate, I discovered upon opening the smokebox door a hole in the cylinder almost as big as a saucer. Harold immediately failed the engine and summoned a replacement from Ryde shed.

Sometime later on No. 32 *Bonchurch,* again with Driver Harold Lacey at the regulator, we encountered another problem. We were entering Haven Street down the gradient when a spindle rod broke and as a result the valve wasn't being pushed to and fro in the steam chest. It sounded as if the engine had shut off steam at 75% cut off on the reversing lever. As soon as we arrived at Haven Street, I had to extinguish the fire and dispose of the burning coal at the side of the track. This time we obtained help from Newport shed who sent an engine to tow us and the train into Newport.

Quite often Harold would spend some time teaching the fireman odd things about the craft of being an engine driver. I recall as soon as we entered Medina Wharf on E1 tanks he would offer me the regulator, and take over my shovel. This basic shunting practice was to prove invaluable in later life, as it gave me confidence to drive locomotives out on the main line.

As a passed fireman, I was called upon to deputise for Driver Charlie Humphries on numerous occasions. I recall on one such occasion we were allocated an E1 tank to work a Medina Wharf to Ryde St John's coal freight train. Charlie's regular fireman, Gerald Coombes used to look after Charlie very well. As we set off from Medina Wharf this E1 tank, which I think was No. 3 *Ryde,* began to shake and rattle giving Gerald and myself a really rough ride on the footplate. As I shot down the long straight on the approach to Haven Street, the lever and cab fittings were continuing to vibrate. I turned around to see young Fireman Coombes tightening up the nuts and bolts, such was his dedication to the job. Gerald was also renowned in steam days as a great wit. Shortly after I got married, I was waiting in number four platform at Ryde Pier Head aboard my locomotive. My wife had prepared me some rock cakes which I decided to share with the seagulls. Gerald came across the footplate and said, "Look at that one. It's knocked his head off. It must have been Hazel's rock cakes".

I worked with Gerald Coombes over the summer season one year. We would take it in turns to drive and fire as we were both passed men. The engine we were allocated that summer was No. 20 *Shanklin.* For some unknown reason the second big valve on this engine was always hard. Gerald's technique when driving was to

'punch it' to achieve that maximum power. One morning we were working the 6.46am, from Ventnor to Ryde on No. 20 and Gerald drove on this return trip. Approaching Sandown, Gerald punched her up in to second valve and she was really barking and making enough noise to wake up all the local residents. Now who should be waiting for us to pass in the siding at Sandown but Fireman Ron Brett and my regular driver, Bill Vallender on No. 17 *Seaview.* Ron was up on the bunker pushing some coal down and paused to look up as we passed while Bill stopped what he was doing to see whatever was happening.

Ron Brett

I recall this occasion as if it were yesterday. Bill just stood in disbelief observing what his regular footplate companion was up to! It's strange I would always deputise for Pete whether firing or driving right up to the end of steam.

Arthur Budden

It is all such a long time ago since I started at Ryde St John's Road and yet I can remember commencing work in October 1945 quite clearly. My first allotted job was cleaning the engines during the night shift. Looking back, this must have been to see just how keen we new boys were. After three or four months of cleaning, I was sent out to fire for Driver Percy Toogood. Unfor-

Above: **Passed Man Ron Brett left and Fireman Ron Mew prepare to depart from Ryde St John's Road with a train for Shanklin in September 1966.** *Rod Hoyle*

Below: **Fireman Ron Brett (left) and Driver Mike Tucker smile for the camera at Ryde shed in 1949. Their engine, No. 23 *Totland* looks resplendent in its new coat of British Railways black livery.** *R. Brett Collection*

tunately, National Service then interrupted my railway career between 1947 and 1949. Upon return to Ryde shed after demob, I was welcomed back by Percy Toogood who asked me to fire to him as his regular man on No. 21 *Sandown.* We got on very well and I stayed with him until 1956. After Percy retired, Eddie Prangnell

Above: **Late running by a Ventnor train at Smallbrook Junction on 8th August 1964 has caused the 'down' Ventnor train to be brought to a stand at the 'down' inner home signal. Fireman Tony Toogood, complete with his distinctive black woolly hat, looks out from the footplate of the stationary locomotive and prepares to jibe his colleagues on the approaching late running train.**

G. M. Kichenside

Below: **A period piece picture of O2 class tank No. 21 *Sandown* passing Smallbrook Junction with a four-coach train from Newport and Cowes. Signalman Vic Hailes, seen collecting the token, dates the picture as circa 1950. Note the lower quadrant lattice signals and crestless locomotive. One wonders if Fireman Arthur Budden was at work on his regular engine when the photograph was taken.**

J. R. G. Griffiths

Passed Man Ron Brett ponders over bygone days of steam whilst waiting at Shanklin station on 31st December 1966. This was Ron's last turn of duty on steam locomotives on the Island.

Peter J. Relf

became my regular driver and his hallmark was to polish 21's cab interior to perfection.

Now Driver Toogood wasn't just a driver he was a real engineman who loved his work. He knew No. 21 *Sandown* inside out. Sometimes after a turn of duty we returned to Ryde shed with a couple of hours to spare. Instead of setting off home early, Percy would ask me

to help him pack one of *Sandown's* glands or sweep a tube out. At the time I resented this work, but now I see in hindsight it made good sense to look after your engine and take pride in it.

Like all footplate crews, we did on occasions encounter problems. I recall setting off from Brading with a two-coach train to Bembridge, when we encountered difficulty in even moving off. Percy opened her regulator, but we didn't move forward an inch. He closed it and repeated the process with no success. All we could feel was the engine rising up on one side, so we climbed down to investigate the cause of our problems. To our amazement we discovered that the brake rod had become uncoupled and was burying itself in the wooden sleeper. Therefore, when we went to move, the locomotive would just lift up into the air.

As I got to know my driver, I realised what a lively sense of humour he had. He somehow acquired the nickname of 'Ducker' Toogood, but the origin of this I never discovered. Much of the object of Driver Toogood's humour was Ryde based guard, Tom Courtenay. On one particular turn, the Ventnor Mail train, we would arrive at Ryde Pier Head, run around the train and set back in number 2 platform with six vans. After uncoupling two vans for the Cowes train we would pull forward and propel our remaining coaches into number 1 platform ready for our departure for Ventnor. Whilst waiting to move forward from number 2 to number 1 platform I looked out to see Tom Courtenay showing a green light. The signal meant ease up. We both knew full well what Tom really wanted but Percy eased up No. 21 *Sandown* according to Tom's signal not once, but twice! Poor old Tom then gave us a white light signal and so we then moved forward and made our way into platform 1. This sequence of events was repeated on several occasions after this, and Tom never understood the ruse.

There were also many amusing sights to see whilst working on the Island railways. One morning I watched Driver Jack Sturgess preparing his beloved No. 22 *Brading*. He was oiling around with his feeder and he climbed up into 22's cab, opened the regulator, in order to move forward a shade for him to get at the rest of the motion for oiling. However, nothing happened as she did not have enough pressure in her steam chest. Jack then wandered back into the shed to find a pinch bar to move the engine forward.

When Jack returned he saw to his horror his 'pride and joy' setting off up the yard under her own steam. He had apparently forgotten to close the regulator and screw down the brake again and whilst in the shed old 22 had built up some steam. It was so funny watching poor Jack Chase after his runaway engine. Luckily, he caught up with her before she could do any damage.

Now I was one who liked to have a bit of fun myself, and so one day when I was given a bag of powdered sulphur I devised a plan. I crept into the cleaner's cabin where there were several of them sleeping in chairs, on tables and so on, and I quietly sprinkled my yellow sulphur on to their fire. I then returned back to the safety of the footplate of my No. 21 *Sandown*. Shortly afterwards we had to set off shed but . . . as we set back through the points towards Ryde Pier my eyes caught sight of Ray Lewns, Don Saunders, Ron Brett and others tearing out of the hut. Now these chaps were fresh out of the Army and they knew exactly who was responsible. If they had caught me, well!

After passing out for driving in 1954, I couldn't wait to take an engine out on my own. One morning at 2.15am, I arrived at Ryde shed to work the Ventnor Mail train with Driver Percy Toogood. Unfortunately, our regular engine, No. 21 *Sandown* was in for boiler washout and we were given a spare engine, No. 23 *Totland* I believe. The locomotive was in a terrible state with coal dust because it had just been lit up, filth covered the gauge glasses. One of the cleaners shouted up to me that I had just missed a driving turn on engine No. 19 *Osbourne* as Driver Arnold "Stooge" Nye had not turned up for work. He informed me that his passed fireman, John Perkis, had taken her out to work the Cowes Mail train. As luck would have it John Perkis was junior to me and therefore this turn of duty was mine for the taking. I looked up and John was waiting at the dummy signal for the 'right-away'. Quickly, I ran as fast as my legs would carry me and claimed my first driving turn. John therefore fired to me and the cleaner who was helping him returned to take over my duty for the day – beginning with cleaning up the mess on the spare engine, No. 23 *Totland!*

As a rule, Driver Percy Toogood insisted on the footplate of his regular engine, No. 21 *Sandown*, being kept 'spick and span'. He also liked the coal dust kept down to a minimum by watering the coal in the bunker. All did not go well on one occasion at Ventnor as we were to discover later. We had arrived in a heavy rain storm and the clouds above the downs were black. After running around our carriages, we had time for a cup of tea in the refreshments room. Ten minutes passed and we returned to the footplate of No. 21. I picked up my shovel and opened the bunker flap to put in a few shovel fulls of coal into 21's firebox. As soon as I opened the bunker flap, out poured a torrent of black dusty water which deposited itself all round the cab floor. Apparently, the rain water from a leaking platform canopy gutter had just poured into our coal bunker during our absence. For most of the journey home to Ryde we had to sit up on the boxes to keep our feet dry and clean! We just looked at each other and laughed.

Summer Saturdays on the Island were pretty hectic and every available engine was required. On one Saturday morning, all that was left for me to drive was an ex-works engine which was out for its first run since a major overhaul. I was informed by the fitter, Wally Herbert, that we would have to go easy with her as the engine's bearings had not been given an opportunity to be run in. Our first turn was from Ryde Pier Head to Cowes. It wasn't long before the side rods were screeching and at Newport I felt they were hot. My fireman 'Long Jim' Arnott passed down some thick oil to pack the boxes. This helped, but upon return to Ryde Pier it was back to square one. Bob Menzies, the Locomotive Running Foreman, happened to be on the platform and I had a word with him about our troubles. We also discovered that a bogie bearing was warm. He asked me to climb down under the engine to see if the metal had run out. Luckily it hadn't so Mr Menzies gave me the all clear to run down to Sandown and back before returning to shed. Upon return to Ryde shed, I discovered that the white metal in the bogie bearing had now run out and so it was 'back into the works' for that particular locomotive.

A few weeks later I was given an O2 tank running bunker first to Ventnor. This was unusual for me and I didn't relish the prospect of working 'bunker first' to Ventnor with an inexperienced fireman. Nevertheless, I thought I would give 'Long Jim' Arnott a chance. He was as keen as mustard and I noted what a lot of hard work shovelling he was putting in. Before we commenced our ascent of Apse Bank from Shanklin, we had to wait for a train to pass us from Wroxall. Jim opened up the firebox doors and reached for the straight dart from the tray. His idea was to place this instrument into the firebox to lift the fire and allow more oxygen into the furnace. Before he did this manoeuvre, I peered into the firebox, and a good job I did too. If he had lifted that fire the brick arch would have dropped down as it was heaped full of coal.

At the end of the Summer service, I returned to firing my regular engine, No. 21 *Sandown,* with Driver Percy Toogood. On one occasion, I had to fire to my opposite turn of duty driver, Harry Linnington. This gentleman had a very strict regime and would treat his regular fireman John "Googie" Withers almost like a boy. His ploy was to carry a red glass plate and keep peering into the firebox and inform his fireman about any holes that appeared. He kept this glass plate in the bottom of a Gladstone bag. I was determined not to have any truck from Driver Linnington and so while he was oiling around the locomotive, I caught hold of this Gladstone bag and banged it onto the opposite side of *Sandown* to which he was oiling. I heard the delightful sound of smashing glass, and with that I knew my day would be clear of criticism.

Generally, I had a good working relationship with my regular driver however. Percy Toogood used to love reading Dickens novels. He would very often quote Dickens' work or burst into poetic song. In those days, we would meet lots of girls in our travels around the Island railways and I had my fair share of girlfriends. One day Driver Toogood came out with the verse, "Oh what a tangled web we weave when first we practice to deceive." As we came out into the light from Ventnor Tunnel I realised what Percy meant. There on Ventnor station platform were two different girls who had come to meet me at the same time! There was one special girl who I used to wave to at Sandown every time we passed on No. 21. Eventually, we met and now that girl is none other than my wife.

It was during this period of time that I began to appreciate what wonderful men worked alongside me on the Island railways. I was courting at the time, and arranged with the driver of the 10.30pm Ventnor–Ryde goods train to be picked up at Shanklin, as the last passenger train back to Ryde left an hour prior to this. True to form Driver Fred Salter, who was on loan from Fratton, pulled into the station with two wagons and a brake van on behind. I climbed aboard and we set off. As we passed Smallbrook Junction signal box, Driver Salter suddenly remembered he hadn't given the staff to the signalman. He quickly threw it back towards the little wooden box. Unfortunately, the signalman had to spend a couple of hours looking for it in the undergrowth. The beauty of it was that nothing official was ever said about this incident – this was how it was on the Island railways in those days.

It was very rare that we had a Locomotive Inspector come across to the Isle of Wight to see us. On one occasion at Ryde Pier Head we had such a visit from one of these gentlemen. He climbed up on to the footplate of *Sandown* and chatted merrily to Driver Toogood. As departure time arrived he peeped into 21's firebox and discovered that I had only three inches of red glowing fire. He realised that the next few minutes would mean some heavy firing on my behalf and he decided to make a quick escape, before I offered him a chance to show how it should be done.

There was one thing which we all enjoyed doing in those days and that was having a good yarn with the staff at the country stations. This was all right as long as it didn't interfere with railway business. I recall that on one occasion Signalman Unstead and myself were merrily chatting at Wroxall. When we first entered the station I gave him the Shanklin–Wroxall staff and he exchanged this for the Wroxall–Ventnor single line staff. As our conversation drew to a close we again exchanged staffs and had it not been for the observant eye of Driver Toogood we would have both been in trouble. Luckily he spotted our mistake before we set off to Ventnor.

Andy Ross

Like so many before me, I began my railway career as a cleaner at Newport shed, on 3rd September 1945. It wasn't long before I became a fireman, but on 5th June 1947 I was released from the railway to join the Army for National Service, as conscription was then the order of the day. After demob in July 1949, I returned to the Island and commenced work straight away as a fireman with Driver Harold Lacey on engine No. 28 *Ashey.* Not long afterwards I passed my exams to become a 'passed fireman'.

One incident stands out in my mind from those days while working on the Merstone Junction to Ventnor West branch with Driver Len J. Harvie. We sometimes worked a freight to Sandown on this duty, but on this particular day there was no work so we stayed down at Merstone in the sidings. With time to kill I pulled the fire back under the door and sat in the train. My driver made himself comfortable and dropped off to sleep while I was reading my usual 'western' novel. At about 4pm I returned to the engine to push the fire over the box as we had to leave at 4.20pm with the next push-pull service train. To my astonishment the fire was as near out as it could be. I told the driver but he didn't believe me and was laughing until he climbed up onto the footplate and looked in the firebox. The adjectives he came out with are not for printing as they would burn the paper. Driver Len Harvie then turned to me, "You let the fire out so you had better tell the signalman". Needless to say the train was cancelled. On reaching the platform and going to the signal box, I had never seen so many people waiting to go to Ventnor West. We did

Above: **Fireman Hugh Snow stands behind his driver Arthur Turner on "Terrier" tank No. 8 Freshwater at Ventnor West.**
Bill Lewis

Above: **Left Bill Lewis, centre Derek Cusons, right Fireman Hugh Snow all on the running plate of No. 8 *Freshwater* at Ventnor West.**
Bill Lewis

manage to get some steam up again and crawled up the siding under the trees. Here we tore down a wooden fence and gathered bits of dead fir trees. Somehow we managed to build up enough steam for the next trip. The outcome of all this was that we both received a reprimand, which was a 'light judgement' as it was taken into consideration the supply of coal on the engine was

mostly dust. A few days later a cartoon from the Daily Mirror newspaper was left for us by a mate at Newport shed, Fireman John Chambers. The cartoon caption read, "Anyone got a match . . . our fire's gone out?"

Now the Island footplate crews who worked at Newport depot in steam days all have a tale to tell about hitting a crossing gate, and I'm no exception. One foggy morning I set off from Newport with Driver Harold Lacey aboard our regular engine *Ashey.* Running down into Ningwood, shortly before Calbourne, there was a level crossing called Pound Crossing with the usual gates worked by the keeper. On this morning the crossing keeper must have overslept. It was so foggy that it was impossible to see more than half the length of the engine. Harold kept shouting across from his driving position on the right of the footplate, "Can you see the gates yet, Andy?" I looked as hard as I could out into the thick fog from the left hand side of the O2's cab, but could see only its Westinghouse pump and Drummond chimney. Eventually we did find those crossing gates with an almighty crash. Harold's classic comment was, "We've

Left: **Left to right Derek Cusons, Bill Lewis's sister, Fireman Hugh Snow and Bill Lewis, standing on the running plate of No. 8 *Freshwater* at Ventnor West.**
Bill Lewis

2486A/252

BRITISH TRANSPORT COMMISSION

G. H. R. GARDENER
Assistant for Isle of Wight
Assistant Representing
Mechanical & Electrical Engineer
Motive Power Superintendent
District Traffic Superintendent, Woking
Telephone
NEWPORT 2429

BRITISH RAILWAYS

ASSISTANT FOR ISLE OF WIGHT

SOUTHERN REGION

NEWPORT STATION

ISLE OF WIGHT

Our Reference   LS1/...B.

Your Reference

6th February,1956.

Passed Fireman A.Ross.
NEWPORT.

Dear Sir,

                CLOSURE OF BRANCH LINES.ISLE OF WIGHT.

        In accordance with Clause 14(a) of the Promotion
Scheme, I have to advise you that in consequence of the
closure of the Newport-Sandown Branch Line, you have now
become redundant in your grade at Newport Depot.

        Please advise me within the stipulated time, viz:-
seven days, your decision with regard to transfer to another
depot on the Region in accordance with Clause 14 of the
Promotion Scheme.

                    Yours truly,

found them mate!" Due to the circumstances neither Harold nor I ever heard a thing about the damage caused.

With the closure of the Newport–Merstone–Sandown line in 1956 I was made redundant, and reluctantly decided to move to Basingstoke where a passed fireman's position awaited me. From then on my steeds were Bulleid 'West Country' Pacifics, 'Lord Nelsons', 'King Arthurs' and other such engines, but my heart remained with the little O2 tank engines on the Isle of Wight railways, and the mates I left behind.

Hugh Snow

It was October 1945, and on the Isle of Wight the Southern Railway reigned supreme. There were two locomotive sheds in operation at this time, at St John's Road, Ryde, and at Newport, the hub of the Island railway network. It was at this time, I joined the Southern Railway as an engine cleaner at Newport.

My first memories are of the old chap who used to give out our daily allocation of cleaning material, a can of oil, some cotton waste and eight or ten cloths. This gentleman's name was Arthur Cassell, but he had the nickname of 'Lyndoe' – quite why I never discovered. We 'nippers' would not dare to call him 'Lyndoe' to his face or we would likely receive a clip around the ears. Surprisingly, I thoroughly enjoyed working on the night shift at Newport shed. There would be about nine or ten of us and we would start cleaning the rows of O2, E1 and "Terrier" tanks at about 11.30pm, when the last of the engines returned to shed. We would work from then until 2am, when we would go to our cabin and have our sandwiches. If a cleaner happened to miss cleaning any part of a locomotive, the Shed Chargeman whose name was Charlie Joiner, would come around to the cabin. Out you go, whether or not you had finished your sandwiches, and you would have to clean that part again. If you had done your cleaning properly it was possible to get your head down until about 6am.

Many other interesting characters worked at Newport shed, including Jim Pointer, a heavily built man who used to bunker the engines with coal using shovels only. Likewise another colourful character was George Dew who was a retired driver whose job in Newport shed was light labouring. He was a good friend of fellow shed labourer Joe Read. One morning Joe overslept and one of the cleaners was sent round to his terrace house to knock him up. The young cleaner could not make Joe hear, so he tried the door and went in. He discovered Joe fast asleep in his bed and swore blind that when he woke Joe up, he just got out of bed, put his hat on, and walked out of the door with him to the shed.

After completing one's time as a cleaner, you usually went out on a firing turn to Medina Wharf. This was a very easy job as it was only three and a half miles each way and a bit of shunting in between. An E1 0-6-0 Brighton tank engine was usually provided for this work, and the two drivers on 'Wharf duty' when I was allocated to this duty were 'Rubbles' Coleman and Tom 'The Doctor' Stanbury. Tom's speciality was the repair of alarm clocks and medicine – hence his title, 'Doctor'. If you told Tom you were not well he would ask you what the symptoms were and he would return the next day with the cure. I don't know what the mixture was but most railwaymen felt worse afterwards. If you wanted an alarm clock Tom would also oblige.

Next to Medina Wharf was the local rubbish tip where the dust carts from the Cowes area used to dispose of their loads. If it was quiet at the Wharf, and there was little shunting to be done, the usual thing to do was to go over to the rubbish tip to see what 'treasures' could be uncovered. On one such occasion I became enlightened as to the source of Tom's alarm clocks. On our way back to Newport the footplate of the E1 tank had a neat pile carefully stacked in the corner.

There were some amusing incidents to witness in the day to day running of the Island lines – I remember one such happened on a Saturday afternoon. We had an E1 tank to shunt a few empty wagons and a brake van to what was called Freshwater Yard which was at the rear of the brewery. My driver, Ron 'Spud' Hayter, was requested by the shunter Alec Woodford to "Hit her up" for a loose shunt. Alec climbed back up on to the LSWR Road van and Driver Hayter opened the regulator of the E1 tank engine until the buffers made contact with those of the Road Van, which shot off around the curve and out of sight at 30 mph. Suddenly, we heard a loud crash. We both looked at each other on the footplate and burst out laughing. After a few seconds 'Spud' Hayter opened the regulator again and we went around to see if the shunter was O.K. He came out of his van limping, but as black as old Nick! Apparently, he had hit the stop buffer-blocks at the end of the siding, before he could get the brake on and as he fell over all the ashes came out of the stove, covering him from head to toe!

My first rostered firing duty was in the summer of 1947, with Driver Fred Radford who was an ex-Nine Elms shed fireman. With Fred you always did things properly on his regular engine, No. 28 *Ashey*. You did *not* touch the locomotive's fire while you were standing in a station as this could create smoke. Another of Fred's taboos was not to let the engine blow off steam in a station, especially Newport and Ryde Pier Head where the passengers would be unable to hear the tannoy broadcasts. Driver Radford also kept a small strip of metal that he used to place between the firebox doors, so that when the doors were closed the fire could draw a small amount of air from above and burn the coal

more efficiently. At night Fred used to carry one of the spare plates that they used during the black-out in wartime, in order to cut out the glare from the fire. Although I did not like working with Fred Radford at first, by the end of the summer I really enjoyed it and no young lad could have had a better start as a fireman, he was a first class tutor.

Shortly after this I was paired up with Charlie 'Liver' Harvey, but just where he got the nickname 'Liver' from I never knew. Driver Harvey was a great one for his beer and 'baccy'. He used to grow his own tobacco for smoking and chewing. Looking back now it was a disgusting habit, spitting tobacco from the cab of our engine.

My next regular driver was Jim Stone and his regular engine was No. 30 *Shorwell*. I recall she was freshly painted black and although she did not look glamorous, *Shorwell* did steam freely. This was used to great advantage on the Ryde–Ventnor line with six coaches packed with holiday-makers on a summer Saturday. The following summer I was promoted to the Branch Gang on the Ventnor West–Merstone Junction branch line. Our regular engines on the branch were two Brighton "Terrier" tanks, Nos 8 *Freshwater* and 13 *Carisbrooke*. My regular driver for the summer was Arthur Turner, a Devon man who came to the Isle of Wight from Barnstaple MPD. We operated the branch trains on the 'push and pull' system, with one coach and engine for the winter timetable and two carriages for the summer. Our duties also included some freight trains on this line, using the same engine in between passenger services. This freight work included coal to Ventnor West for the hospital and during the winter we took sugar beet from Godshill siding to Merstone Junction. These sugar beet wagons were then shunted on the return Ventnor goods and thence to Medina Wharf to be loaded into boats for the mainland. Incidentally, the Ventnor West branch train was the only corridor train on the Isle of Wight, because the stations between Merstone and Ventnor West were un-manned and therefore the train guard doubled as a ticket collector as well.

In the winter months when the evenings were dark the train carried hurricane lamps, and it was the guard's task to fill and light them and put two lamps on the stations at Godshill, Whitwell and St Lawrence. These hurricane lamps were taken down by the guard on the last train of the night, the 7.57pm from Ventnor West. Whilst at work on the branch, like other railway staff, I got to know all our regular passengers by name and one particular lady from Whitwell used to go shopping in Ventnor every Friday morning. She always had a bag of cakes for the driver, fireman and guard on the return journey.

It was on the Ventnor West branch that I met the girl who later became my wife. We had a two hour lay-over at Merstone in the afternoon, from 2.20pm until 4.20pm, and if there was no freight working I would nip across a couple of fields to her house for a crafty cup of tea.

Usually on Mondays and Thursdays the late shift would take the gas coal out on the bridge at Newport over the River Medina, ready for unloading for the gas works. As soon as the last train from Ryde to Cowes came into Newport station at 10.06pm, we would propel

The copper-capped chimney of No. 13 *Carisbrooke* and vintage car in the car park all add interest to this panoramic view of Ventnor West station, which was taken from the stop blocks.

J. R. G. Griffiths

the wagons of coal out onto the bridge, and Bill Eldridge, Jim Hewitt and their team would set about emptying all the wagons – and this, after a full day shift at work. Sadly, this scene has now disappeared and all we have left are the memories of those wonderful days.

Don Pegg

The 28th January 1946 will always stand out in my memory as a turning point in my life, for it was on this day that I joined the railways as an engine cleaner. From March until May 1946 I was sent out to work on the Brading–Bembridge branch as a fireman with Driver Fred 'Cock' Hilditch. Little did I know that in later years Fred would become my father-in-law, for after taking water for our thirsty locomotive at Brading, one day I returned to the footplate to discover Fred's daughter Joyce. From then on until I was promoted, Joyce would bring cakes for Fred and me to Brading station, which she made at her cookery class.

Driver Fred Hilditch was originally from London hence his nickname – 'Cock'. His grandfather was Station Master at Woking and his father was Storeman at Nine Elms locomotive shed. Driver Hilditch came across to the Isle of Wight in 1928 and was based at Ryde St John's Road shed. Whilst working with Fred Hilditch on the Bembridge branch aboard engine No. 14 *Fishbourne,* he would often recall his memories. During the Second World War Fred told me how his train was machine gunned and his driver, Charlie Humphries drove the locomotive and carriages into Ryde Esplanade tunnel

until it was safe to come out. When Fred worked on the Bembridge branch he was often in Sheila's Cafe just outside Bembridge station for his refreshment break. On one such occasion, on Grand National Day in 1947, Fred heard that a horse was running by the name of Sheila's Cottage. He advised all his colleagues on the railway to back it and as luck would have it, the horse won!

In July, 1946 I was up-graded to fireman and so sadly Driver Fred 'Cock' Hilditch and I parted company on the footplate, although I still saw a good deal of him as I was now courting his daughter Joyce. My new footplate companion was Driver Alf Goodson and our regular engine was No. 22 *Brading,* which was to be our regular locomotive for the next twelve years. There was no better engine than 22, and her cab and brass polished to perfection every day. She was a picture to look at and our opposite shift crew on the engine, under the watchful eye of Driver Jack Sturgess took a similar pride in the locomotive's appearance.

Our fine locomotive, *Brading* was a challenge when you consider the different types of coal we had to burn in her firebox, ie steam, household, briquettes and even anthracite, on one occasion. On the latter occasion, I was struggling all the way from Ryde trying to maintain steam. By the time we entered Shanklin at the foot of Apse Bank we came to a full stop. There was just a mere 60 lb of steam registering on 22's gauge and the water was in the bottom nut. The guard came up with his hand lamp and I remember inviting him to shine his lamp in the firebox to see if he could find any signs of the fire. It took me a full 45 minutes to clean out the treacle like clinker, before I could get enough steam to proceed to Ventnor.

In February, 1952 I remember being stuck on 22's footplate all day during a severe gale, which forced waves from the high tide across Ryde Pier. In fact there were

Right: **Driver Fred 'Cock' Hilditch looks back along the train at Wroxall to make sure that all the doors are safely closed before continuing on the last leg of the journey to Ventnor. The Southern Railway notice to passengers and the lower quadrant Southern Railway lattice signal add period interest.**
J. R. G. Griffiths

Below: **Fireman Ken Simmonds ensures that the tanks of O2 No. 35 *Freshwater* are adequately topped up with water, while Driver Jack Sewell attends to the water column control. Sadly, this picture was taken on 14th September 1952, the day the Ventnor West branch closed.**
Malcolm Jefferies/Bill Lampard Collection

two trains trapped in the platforms at Ryde Pier. We were on No. 22 *Brading* with a train for Ventnor whilst waiting in the other platform was Driver Harry 'Oh Ah' Linnington and Fireman John 'Googie' Withers on No. 21 *Sandown* with a train for Newport and Cowes. We both closed the dampers on engines 21 and 22 and just sat and waited for the storm to subside, while we kept the fire going with the blowers full on.

We had our laughs on old 22, like the time Driver Alf Goodson took his shoe off to shake out some coal dust. The trouble was that we were on the end of Ryde Pier and his shoe slipped out of his hand. It splashed in the salt water below and promptly sank down to the sea bed. Poor Alf was hopping about for the rest of the shift.

Now Ryde Pier was a bogie place for Alf and engine No. 22. One day we were shunting some vans at the end

The photographer has risen early to capture this train on film as it is the 7.40 am from Ryde Pier Head, double-headed by No 28 *Ashey* and an unidentified O2 tank engine. The train is seen approaching Smallbrook Junction. *H. P. Mason*

of Ryde Pier Head when we knocked the last one off in platform 3. We returned light engine back to St John's Road loco shed. Upon arrival, the Foreman, Reg Megget said to Alf, "You have put a van up on the blocks!" Driver Goodson argued that he most certainly had not knocked a van off the rails and added that he was nowhere near it at the time. All the same, we had to return on *Brading* to pull the van off the stop blocks. Luckily, it dropped back on the rails with no damage caused.

In 1958, I left Ryde for promotion as a driver in the dual link at Bognor Regis and finally ended up at Littlehampton as a motorman driver.

Ken Simmonds and Ray Knapp

Ken Simmonds

After demobilisation from the Navy, I returned to the Isle of Wight with an uncertain view as to my future career. At first I worked for a spell at Whites, but this wasn't for me. Then I had the good fortune to meet an old friend, Ron Brett, who suggested I join him on the railways. I wandered down to Ryde St John's Road shed and spoke to Mr Meggett and joined the newly formed British Railways as an engine cleaner.

A few months passed and I was given the opportunity to fire on engine No. 14 *Fishbourne,* on the Brading–Bembridge branch with a variety of drivers: Alf Tester, George Cammell, O.P. 'Rabbits' Vallender to name but a few. It was a diabolical turn as it always involved the late turn of duty with thirteen return trips. At the time, lady luck favoured me and a fireman's post became vacant at Newport shed. My application was successful and I went on to greener pastures!

I will always remember that first morning as a fireman at Newport. I reported for duty at 3.25 in the morning and introduced myself to my driver, Tom Stanbury. With a good fire in the box, we were ready to set off to Medina Wharf for some shunting. Suddenly, the Shed Foreman appeared and asked me to step in as fireman on the Freshwater Mail train, as the duty fireman, Monty Harvie had overslept. Immediately, I left what I was doing and climbed up onto No. 29 *Alverstone* where I saw an angry Driver Jack Sewell was awaiting my assistance at the shovel. It was a mixed train of passenger coaches, vans for the newspapers and parcels and a few odd wagons. Now the driver didn't speak a word to me until we were almost into Yarmouth. "Handbrake boy, handbrake!" shouted Driver Sewell. He then asked me to open the gates. What gates I thought? I climbed down from the footplate of *Alverstone* and strolled along to the front buffers. Sure enough, just an inch in front of the buffers was a set of wooden gates. After opening the gates we continued on forward the train's length and the guard then closed the crossing gates behind the last carriage. Nothing like this at Ryde I thought!

Ray Knapp

My first contact with the Island railways was at the age of three and a half. I climbed up Towngate Viaduct which is on the Freshwater line just leaving Newport, and fell off. Luckily, I was rescued by 'Ginger' Fisk, the Foreman who rushed me to the local hospital. Years passed and I worked on a farm which had fields either side of the railway on the Cowes side of Newport. It was here I met Mr Bell the Foreman at Newport station who used to help out on the farm at odd occasions. He kindly offered me a job on the railway which I decided to accept. Hence at the age of 21 in 1950, I commenced work as a cleaner of Newport shed.

Like Ken, I had the opportunity to go out firing on odd occasions but we were mostly restricted to Medina Wharf. During the summer season cleaners were quite often called upon to help fire on the main Cowes-Newport-Ryde or Newport-Sandown or Newport-Freshwater lines. When on the Newport-Ryde section we of course had to pass Smallbrook Junction. The cleaners were instructed to throw the Ashey-Smallbrook single line token on the signal box steps if the Smallbrook signalman was giving a token to the Ventnor line trains on the other side of the signal box – thus alleviating an unnecessary stop. Now one winter when Smallbrook Junction signal box was closed a cleaner colleague was called upon to assist with a firing turn to Ryde from Newport. As the locomotive passed Smallbrook box, the keen young lad reached out of the cab and hurled the single line token towards the wooden signal box. "Hey, hey, boy!" yelled the driver. "What's your game?" The cleaner replied that his actions were according to instructions regarding Smallbrook. From this date we were all given new instructions for Smallbrook Junction which was closed during the winter season, ie hold on to that token until St John's Road was reached.

Ken Simmonds

Looking back, those early firing turns as a cleaner were an ideal learning experience to familiarise one's self with track and signalling as well as the controls of each type of locomotive.

Ray Knapp

It was possible for a driver not to be totally familiar with each of the three types of locomotive in service on the Isle of Wight. For instance, one particular driver comes to mind – a Ryde man by the name of George 'Seagull' Reeves. He was only accustomed to working on the O2 and "Terrier" tank locomotives. Therefore, when he was presented with one of the four Newport based Brighton E1 tank locomotives to haul a freight up to Ryde, he was baffled and confused by the positioning of the controls in the cab. I climbed up into the cab and gave 'Seagull' a quick briefing on the main controls as they were totally in reverse to those on an O2. For some reason, I had to return to the Newport Shed Foreman's office and left the Ryde driver to reverse back to the coal stage. As he did so, 'Seagull' forgot where the brake handle was located. Too late – "thud, crash, bang". When I came out to investigate what the noise was our engine had run into two dead locomotives positioned just beyond the coal stage.

Ken Simmonds

Engine No.24 *Calbourne* was a marvellous engine and thank goodness she is preserved at Haven Street. I wonder if they have come across a repair to the bunker and roof yet? Perhaps I should explain how this came about for the Isle of Wight Steam Railway's records. One evening we had *Calbourne* out on a run to Cowes and back, but on this occasion Driver Ken West was either off sick or on a rest day. As a replacement, Driver Ken Stevens was driving the locomotive. On the return journey we were heading bunker first to Ryde, and approaching Cement Mills Halt when Ken spotted the silhouette of what he thought was a branch of a tree. It was too late to slow down but Ken applied the brakes. As we approached we made out in the darkness that it was the jib of a crane. The impact with this object ripped through the bunker and caused extensive damage to the roof. Upon arrival at Newport Driver Jack Bradford and Fireman Gerald Coombes took over our duty with No.36 *Carisbrooke*.

Ray Knapp

We all liked to see our engines bright and polished, and the higher-ups on the railways used to like to cover their uniforms with brass braid. Not to be outdone a fireman friend decided to out-do the bosses and match the brass work on the engines – none other than Fred Janaway. He put a brass band around his hat, sewed brass buttons on his bib and braces coat and pockets, finishing off with a copper watch chain. He looked a real treat and we all admired him for his pluck.

When the Queen visited the Island we all had our engines polished up for the day, although Her Majesty did not travel by rail. I remember working back from Ventnor with empty stock and waiting for a 'down' train to pass us at Wroxall. After allowing Driver Ted Dale to pass by us on No.29 *Alverstone*, we were clear for the run down Apse Bank to Shanklin. On this occasion I was the driver and my fireman was Terry Drudge. Although I could see lots of children waiting with flags for the Queen to pass by there was no sign of her and we had to depart. As we set out down the cutting I had second thoughts and applied the Westinghouse brake. At that very moment Her Majesty The Queen passed over Wroxall bridge and so I pulled the whistle for all I was worth and waved. The Queen turned around to

Terry Drudge and myself and gave us an enthusiastic royal wave! Her Rolls-Royce was ordered to slow down and Her Majesty drew the attention of the Duke of Edinburgh to her loyal railway subjects who also gave a wave. To crown it all however, upon return to Ryde depot my fireman received a letter, "We regret your services are no longer required at this engine shed owing to staff redundancies". His only comment was, "If I'd known, I wouldn't have waved at the Queen!"

Ken Simmonds

During my firing days at Newport shed, I used to work with Driver Alec Bailey from time to time. He used to like to clean behind the regulator on the engine, and once or twice we have been going along the line from Freshwater to Newport and Alec has taken off the regulator handle to clean behind it – a rather dangerous practice.

After completing our servicing, Driver 'Seagull' Reeves backed on to the forty-wagon coal train. Guard George Francis blew his whistle and waved his green flag and away we went over the curving viaduct and into Newport Tunnel. "How shall I drive her?" asked Driver Reeves. "Go by instinct," was my reply, "and give her a bit of stick". Now it was mid-August and the embankments were dry and this latter bit of advice was our undoing. Upon arrival at St John's Road, George Francis climbed up onto the footplate to report that from Fairlee Cutting, just outside Newport, to Ashey we had left a trail of fires and the Fire Brigade was now attempting to put them out!

Ken Simmonds

One of my first regular drivers, who must remain nameless for obvious reasons, had a girl friend at Cowes. The custom was as follows. As we entered Cowes station, the signal box was situated on the left-hand side and as the locomotive passed by, 'a rope' would appear from over the fence of one of the adjoining houses. The driver, who is now sadly dead, would then ask me to uncouple the locomotive and run around the train etc., whilst he joined his lady friend for a cup of tea and refreshment. This practice continued for some years, but so far as I know his wife never discovered!

Ray Knapp

One of my regular drivers was Alf Goodson and our regular engine was No.22 *Brading*. We worked opposite turns of duty to Driver 'Mad' Jack Sturgess and Fireman Roy Dyer. At first, we didn't get on until one day we had an almighty argument. From then on we became firm friends until he retired.

I recall one cold dark winter's evening at Ryde Pier Head station I could so easily have perished. We were waiting with a train for Ventnor and I climbed down from the footplate of No.22 *Brading* on the steps leading down from the cab. Upon reaching the bottom I began to descend quickly and it was only the cast iron

railings that saved me from a chilling dip in the arctic-sea below. The previous night they had suffered a storm at Ryde Pier which washed away some of the wooden decking. As I dangled above the lapping waves below, I called out to Driver Goodson for help, but old 22 was blowing off steam and my voice was not audible. It wasn't until Ken West came across from his engine, *Calbourne* to speak to Alf that my presence was missed. Immediately, Ken West and Alf discovered me in my plight and rescued me. Back on *Calbourne*, was one Ken Simmonds who was then her regular fireman!

My favourite engine was No.29 *Alverstone* when driven by Jack Sewell. She would steam freely and pull exceptionally well following her overhaul at Eastleigh after the war. This particular locomotive was always worth an extra coach pulling power in comparison to the other O2 tanks. The E1 tank engines used to have some pulling power compared with the O2s, although their disadvantage was that when hauling passenger trains they would hunt from side to side at speed, giving footplate crews an uncomfortable ride. The roughest locomotive of the four E1 tanks in service on the Island was No.1 *Medina*. Shortly before withdrawal I had a ride on her. *Medina's* wooden floor in the cab was beginning to rot away, and furthermore, when the driver applied the brakes the cylinder which was bolted onto the underside of the floor would lift up. Footplate crews began to complain to the powers that be about the engine's appalling condition and in June 1957 she was withdrawn from service and cut up for scrap.

Ken Simmonds

Right up to the end of steam traction on the Isle of Wight we were proud of the interiors of our cabs. When I was working with Ken West on No.24 *Calbourne*, Ken would always insist that before the engine went in for a washout, the fittings would be oil smeared. The idea of this was to prevent soot smears from dirtying the brass fittings and gauges when the locomotive was lit up from cold following her boiler washout.

Ray Knapp

One driver was even particular about the quality of coal his locomotive burned. Driver Charlie Linnington would regularly pay 6d to the coalman to make sure his O2 tank had the best coal available.

It was sad to see the Island railway lines disappear one by one. In fact, I had to fire on the last train ever between Newport and Freshwater. Our assignment was to take an engine and brake van out to Freshwater and collect all empty wagons placed in the various sidings along the route. In addition to this we were also asked to collect all station seats, signal arms and anything that was of any future use. The driver on this sad occasion was Monty Harvie and we were accompanied in the brake van by Inspector Henry Powers, S&T staff and our guard Reg Seaman. As we pulled away from Yarmouth, I just had to have one last look back and to my surprise I saw Inspector Powers, Guard Seaman and the

Above: **A magnificent portrait picture of No. 32 *Bonchurch* at Freshwater. This was the last green liveried Adams O2 locomotive. Driver Arthur Turner and Fireman Ken Simmonds had the pleasure of being the rostered footplate crew on this engine, which hauled the RCTS Special in May 1952.** *J. R. G. Griffiths*

Below: **Driver Fred 'Cock' Hilditch and Fireman John Millward give a smile to Sir Peter Allen from engine No. 14 *Fishbourne* at Shanklin on a wet summer Saturday in 1953. Sir Peter and another member of the Allen family had just received a footplate ride aboard No. 14 from Ryde Pier Head.** *Sir Peter Allen*

Driver Ray Knapp on engine No. 27 *Merstone* collects the single line token from Porter-Signalman Hughie White at Haven Street, watched by Miss Elizabeth Winter of Fairview Cottage, opposite Haven Street station building. This was one of the last days of operation of the Cowes line as the photograph is dated 19th February 1966.
G. S. Cocks

rest of our passengers chasing the brake van around the curve. It was an amusing sight to remember and a nice note on which to say farewell to the Freshwater line.

John Millward

Originally from Devon, I started on the Island railways at Ryde shed in 1946. With a brief interlude for National Service between 1947 and 1949, I returned to Ryde as a fireman. They were a fine set of lads at the shed and soon fellow fireman and friend John 'Googie' Withers introduced me to his sister-in-law who I later married.

In those early days of Nationalisation, I learnt my trade on the Bembridge branch, which I came to regard as a 'tear and go line' as we operated a virtual non-stop shuttle service twixt Brading and Bembridge. During this immediate post-war period we were all on rationing. The practice was whilst on late turn to halt freight trains in the darkness for "supplementary railway rations". On one such occasion, George Cammell on No.14 *Fishbourne* stopped to acquire milk from the cows in the nearby fields, eggs from some friendly hens and a hat full of mushrooms. A fine footplate meal was had by all!

It was not long before I was given a regular engine to work on, and fire to a regular driver, in the form of No.18 *Ningwood* and Driver Fred 'Cock' Hilditch. Usually it was a good engine, but on one occasion on a summer Saturday at Shanklin the Westinghouse brakes failed completely. The Assistant for the Isle of Wight railways, Mr G.H.R. Gardiner was on board at the time as a passenger. He asked Fred if there was any way we could struggle back to Ryde and keep the service going. Now Fred could never resist a challenge and he told Mr Gardiner to rest easy and he would do his best. He gently opened 18's regulator and we crawled along at a very limited speed using the handbrake only. This proved to be somewhat nerve-racking coming down through Lake past Los Altos Park. Somehow we managed to make it in to St John's Road where Mr Gardiner came up to thank us for carrying on.

On another occasion we were approaching Ryde Pier Head station on *Ningwood* when Driver Hilditch spotted something wrong just ahead of us. Inspector Henry Powers was in the Pier Head signal box operating the levers and inadvertently set the points into the wrong platform, where a train for Cowes was preparing to depart. Fred immediately applied the brakes at the approach to the points. With this the attention of Vic Hailes, the Pier Head box regular signalman, focused on us. Vic knew what he was up to and set us right, but Inspector Powers didn't bat an eye!

One unusual and painful incident comes to mind from the year 1957. Driver Fred Hilditch and I were waiting at Ryde St John's Road to relieve George Cammell on *Ningwood*, who was approaching with a train from Ventnor. As he pulled into the platform the engine cab door was closed and George refused to get off 18's footplate. At that moment a demented passenger ran up to the footplate shouting and screaming at George. He tried to punch George and Fred stepped in with me to protect him. We arrested the passenger but in so doing he gave me a black eye. When the police arrived to take him away, they informed us that this gentleman had escaped from a local psychiatric hospital.

At times I had to relieve on other engines or with other drivers. Here it was possible to see different techniques of driving in action. I recall being asked to help out by firing to Driver O.P. 'Rabbits' Vallender on No.24 *Calbourne*. We were due to relieve Driver Bill Miller and Fireman Bert Lock at Ryde Pier Head. As soon as we took over I looked into *Calbourne's* firebox to see the state of the fire. Unfortunately, Fireman Lock had kept the damper down too long, consequently the coal on the bars was glowing a bluey colour. It was a struggle to get a good head of steam. Driver Vallender's solution was to make *Calbourne* slip and lose her feet on the rails. This action brought some life into the fire.

During the summer season service, Ryde shed often received extra assistance from Fratton shed on the mainland. One summer I was asked to fire to a Fratton driver, Driver Jefferies, on No.23 *Totland*. Naturally enough, the Fratton drivers were always keen to return across the Spithead to their homes. One particular night we arrived on No.23 at the Pier Head station and Driver Jefferies

Driver Denny Snow makes a vigorous start from Ryde St John's Road on a dull 4th January 1964, with the 1.37 pm to Ventnor. Driver Snow has the cylinder cocks open on spare engine No. 16 Ventnor with the regulator fully opened in full forward gear. What a lucky man photographer John Goss must have been to witness this spectacle.

John Goss

asked me if I could do him a favour. He particularly wanted to catch the 9.30pm boat from Ryde to Portsmouth, but the problem was that if he returned on the engine to St John's shed he would miss the boat home. I therefore agreed to help him out, but unfortunately by this time I had thrown out the fire into the sea and pressure was now dropping rapidly. As I opened 23's regulator, running light engine from the Pier, the pressure was 160 lb. As I passed through Ryde Esplanade the pressure was dropping below 100 lb per square inch, but it was downhill into the tunnel. By now, I was wondering about the wisdom of driving and firing on my own. Limping into St John's Road she was just puffing along at 60 lb. Luckily the points for the shed changed before I could stop, so I shut the regulator and pulled the pole back to keep momentum going. I just made it on to the shed. I resolved that "my heart would never rule my head" again with regard to railways!

A few weeks passed and I was still with Driver Jeffer-

ies, but this time we were assigned to work a Sandown-Merstone-Newport-Cowes train, 'around the houses' as this duty was called. With just two coaches behind, what could be easier for a footplate crew? Not so on this occasion. Driver Jefferies and myself at the shovel climbed aboard the footplate of O2 tank No.34 *Newport* (I believe), at Sandown station, in the Newport bay platform. I looked in the bunker to discover that our coal supply was just pure coal dust. Driver Jefferies was used to this type of coal on 'West Country' Pacifics at Fratton, and he advised me to build up a big fire under the firebox door of No.34. After some argument Driver Jefferies exchanged his regulator for my shovel. As we set off around the curve towards Alverstone, steam pressure began to drop considerably. Passing through Newchurch the situation was deteriorating rapidly with injector problems. At Horringford, our speed had dropped to something like running speed. Finally, we limped into Merstone where the weary Driver Jefferies

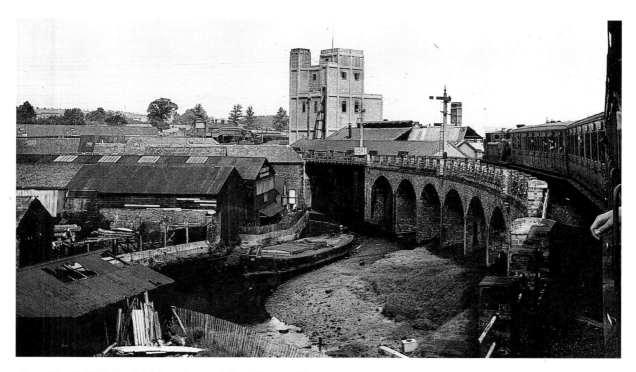

Above: **The R.C.T.S. Special is brought to a halt on Newport Viaduct leading in from Shide, on the Sandown-Merstone-Newport section. The reason for the stop can be seen in the picture as a train is about to depart for Ryde, to be followed by a service train for Sandown. To the left of the train stands a Mew Langton barge awaiting the turn of the tide on the River Medina. The tall building in the centre of the picture is the Newport gas works.** *J. R. G. Griffiths*

Below: **Another view of the R.C.T.S. Special of Sunday, 18th May 1952, this time taken at Newport prior to a locomotive change. The significance here, however, is that the fireman on E1 Class No. 3** *Ryde* **was Dennis Snow and a look back to** *Once Upon A Line, Volume One,* **page 73, shows Fireman Snow on the footplate of No. 3 at Cowes station.** *J. R. G. Griffiths*

readily exchanged the shovel for his regulator. After pausing at Merstone to build up some steam we set off cautiously. The remainder of the journey continued with barely a word passing between us. He never admitted that his Bulleid Pacific firing methods were not right for Island tank engines – our performance on *Newport* said it all.

In 1958, I passed my driver's examinations and was looking forward to a bright future with my own regular engine at Ryde shed. It therefore, came as a great shock when the doctor informed me that I had a colour defect in my eyes! This signalled the end of my ambitions to driving on the main lines twixt Ryde-Cowes and Ventnor. The railway authorities then offered me a driving job strictly within the confines of Ryde locomotive depot, to shunt and prepare engines. This job consisted of working anti-social hours from 11pm until 7am to prepare engines by driving them into the coal stage, oiling up, preparing them for wash-out, and placing the engines into order for the next day's duty.

To the railway enthusiast who reads these words, the engine shed at Ryde was the home for the Island locomotives. I guess it was a place of mystery and excitement where the, ''No Admittance Except On Business'' sign, only acted as a further incentive to get in and have a peep. Yet to me there was little romanticism about working in these draughty and dirty conditions at the time. Looking back the memory of the atmosphere of Ryde shed lingers on – that certain smell and sound is unforgettable.

For the benefit of those who never knew Ryde shed on a summer Saturday, let me here recall a few brief memories. I would arrive for duty at 11pm Friday night which would be the beginning of a hectic few hours. The shed would have up to eight engines under the protection of its corrugated asbestos roof. Outside, the yard would be littered with O2 and E1 locomotives emitting a dull bluey grey smoke haze. The task ahead of fellow workers such as Ted Joyce, Jim Lock the fitter, Jim Hewitt the coalman, myself and others was to prepare fifteen engines for duty for the Saturday service.

At roughly 2am the first set of men would report for duty and prepare their O2 tank for duty 1. They would be followed a quarter of an hour later by another pair of men to crew the engine for duty 2. These two duties were for the Ventnor and Cowes mail trains. The duty 1 locomotive would steam off the shed at 2.50am, pick up the empty coach stock and head towards Ryde Pier Head ready for 4.05am departure to Ventnor. Number 2 duty would follow a quarter of an hour behind. The next couple of hours were the most hectic period as six engines had to be prepared for departure of the depot by 6am. Twenty-six sets of men would have reported for duty throughout the day to operate the intensive summer Saturday service. During the day the various engines would return to shed for coaling, servicing and de-ashing. In those days Ryde shed was just a hive of activity on summer Saturdays with no respite for shed staff.

Sadly, this pattern all came to an end in 1966, with the closure of the Cowes and Shanklin-Ventnor lines. All too soon, the last day of steam operation came and it was a strange feeling to prepare the engines for their last day of operation. Seven engines were made ready, Nos 14 *Fishbourne*, 16 *Ventnor*, 17 *Seaview*, 22 *Brading*, 24 *Calbourne*, 27 *Merstone* and 31 *Chale*. A last special clean for No.14 which was to haul the last train and Nos 24 and 31 which pulled a LCGB special, and that was it – I was redundant.

Dennis A. 'Snowy' Snow

The first thing that I can recall, when I started work at Newport locomotive shed in September 1946 was the smell of hot oil, coal and steam. Once smelt, this distinctive aroma could never be forgotten. My next vivid memory of those early days working as an engine cleaner are of the winter of 1946/1947 when I was given the task of keeping the water columns free of ice. The water columns were located on the station platforms at Newport and beneath each, were 'fire devils', which were a device for keeping the temperature above freezing point. To look at, these 'devils' were constructed in a barrel like shape with four supporting legs and a chimney which carried the heat up to the water columns. My job was to wheel barrows of steam coal from the engine shed to the 'devils' and keep a good fire burning within them. However, that winter the ice covered the whole structure of the water columns and icicles hung right down to the platform, so we fought a losing battle in trying to keep them free of ice.

In June 1947 I went for a two year holiday to the Far East on National Service. When I returned in 1949 I had been made up to fireman. My first driver was Fred Harvey with whom I stayed for approximately six months. We were located in the bottom link and our assignments included shunting the yards at Newport and Medina Wharf along with branch line workings. Then one day, Mr Bale the Foreman at Newport depot called me into his office and allocated me to work with Driver Gerald Groundsell. Our first day at work together was on a late turn of duty working the Cowes-Newport-Merstone-Sandown train service. On the second run to Sandown, our Adams O2 tank and three carriages went straight through Newchurch station. I said to Driver Groundsell, ''We should have stopped at Newchurch''. He replied with a devilish grin, ''That's all right nipper, we will stop on the way back''. I must add that Gerald was one of the nicest railwaymen that one could have wished to work alongside. He was a model engineer and had a tremendous knowledge of all things mechanical. It was therefore sad to hear that within a couple of years Driver Groundsell was put back on shed duties owing to his ill health.

The next driver I worked with was Arthur Turner and our regular engine was No.32 *Bonchurch*. This driver was a nice chap, but he was always moaning about the coal dust on the footplate blowing up his trouser legs. After listening to his complaints for about six weeks, I drew a chalk line in the centre of the footplate whereupon Driver Turner enquired what it was for. I informed him that from then on we would sweep our own halves of the footplate. This stopped his moaning once and for all!

For a short period of time, I worked with Driver Charlie Palmer on No.31 *Chale*, and my lasting impression of this driver is that nothing seemed to worry him. On one occasion we had disposed of No.31 and dropped her down on the coal road at Newport shed for refuelling. We then retired into the shed to wash up before going home. Suddenly, we heard some unpleasant sounds from outside as Nobby Thomas, the coalman, had driven 31 off the road and she had derailed on the points. Charlie's reaction to this was to casually say to me, "Put a red light on the engine so that nobody else runs into her". Then he went off home calling at 'the local' on his way.

During my firing days, I have at some time or other worked with all the Island drivers on all the different locomotives with one exception – Driver 'Mad' Jack Sturgess. However, I did manage to work on 'Mad' Jack's engine, No.22 *Brading*, alongside his opposite shift driver, Alf Goodson. Driver Goodson's regular fireman, Ray Knapp, was away on holiday and I was therefore booked to work on No.22 for about a week. On a return trip from Cowes to Ryde, Alf looked across the footplate at me and remarked that most of the Newport shed firemen he had been allocated to work with were useless! I replied very promptly, "All the Ryde drivers I had been with were also useless!" After that we got on fine.

For the final few years of steam traction on the Isle of Wight I was promoted to a driver. My regular mate at the fireman's shovel was Bob Church and our regular engine at first was No.27 *Merstone*. In those days No.27 had a Drummond boiler and for a former Newport-based man, who was familiar with this type of engine, she was a joy to drive. The Ryde men who were more used to the Adams boilered type O2 tanks experienced some difficulty with the Drummond design and this would often lead to priming through over filling of the boiler. When 27 went into Ryde Works for a general overhaul and reboilering I was reallocated to No.22 *Brading* which also had a Drummond design boiler.

Brading was a superb engine to drive and I have fond memories of her with the exception of an incident that occurred at Ryde Pier Head. It was a scorching summer Saturday at the peak of the summer season in 1965. We arrived at Ryde Pier Head from Ventnor and headed into platform 1 bunker first on *Brading*. The procedure was for us to uncouple from the carriage set and wait until a locomotive had coupled up to the rear of the train. It would then be signalled out to depart for Ventnor. Immediately after the Ventnor bound train had departed we crept down the platform and took water. We then shunted forwards out along the 'down' line towards Ryde and waited just beyond the crossover points, which were exactly opposite Ryde Pier Head signal box. After a few minutes patiently waiting my mate and I heard a click. "Rightaway, Den", shouted the fireman across the cab. Thinking that the points had been changed for us and the dummy signal pulled off, I whistled up and gently opened 22's regulator. Immediately the signalman started to shout, "Stop, stop!" and waved a red flag. It was too late, our rear bogie wheels were off the rails. My fireman had mistook the sound of the click for our dummy signal and point change, but what he had heard was the signal being pulled off on the 'up' line and the points set accordingly. Luckily, the approaching train from Ryde Esplanade was halted.

This incident left No.22 *Brading* derailed for some hours. Chargehand Bill Smith from Ryde Works arrived on the scene to re-rail 22 with a team of fitters, but his first order was, "Put the kettle on for a cup of tea!" Eventually, the Shed Foreman arrived to inspect the damage and Bill got his team to work. Potentially this incident could have resulted in something a lot worse with possibly our engine ending up in the sea below. As the driver in charge, I accepted full responsibility, but I will always be grateful to my colleagues for helping me out of this mess.

This remarkable photograph (taken in colour) shows No. 22 *Brading* with her rear bogie wheels off the rails on the cross-over points on Ryde Pier in the summer of 1965. An account of the incident is described by the driver of the locomotive, Dennis Snow. Pictured here are Cyril Henley of the Signalling & Telegraph Department with his back to the camera looking out to sea and to his right is Passed Cleaner, Paddy Lock, who was 22's fireman on this occasion.

Mike Morant

Left: **No. 22** *Brading* **awaits departure from Ryde Esplanade as a train approaches from Ventnor on 19th February 1966. According to the record, No. 22 is crewed by Driver Snow and Fireman Bob Church, but in this view they are both out of the picture.**

G. S. Cocks

Below: **No. 33** *Bembridge* **blasts her way up Apse Bank with the 5.10 pm Ryde to Ventnor train, seen here in Hyde Cutting on 19th September 1960. Is Driver Snow trying to make up lost time or did he always drive his engines in such an impressive way? Whatever the answer, 33 is certainly making dramatic smoke effects!**

H. P. Mason

Some amusing things were to be seen on the Island railways in steam days. Quite often footplate crews would return from Shanklin and Ventnor with prize pheasants hanging up in the cabs of their O2 tank engines. These game birds would be caught on the single line section between Smallbrook Junction and Brading. Footplate crews would arm themselves with steam coal from the bunkers as they entered this section of line and take aim at anything that moved in Whitefield Woods. Consequently, heavily loaded passenger trains made frequent unofficial stops to collect their engine crew's prize catches. The Operating Authorities tried to curtail this highly irregular going-on and a notice appeared on the rostering/special notices board at Ryde St John's depot. "The practice of throwing fuel at game in Whitefield Woods must cease forthwith!" The practice of throwing fuel did stop – from then on we used stones to aim at the game birds!

Food was always a regular topic of conversation on the lips of Isle of Wight footplate crews. When working as a fireman, it was always a pleasure to work on No.21 *Sandown*, as her driver, Eddie Prangnell, always looked

Above: **Signalman Vic Hailes hands the token to Driver Dennis Snow as he passes by on engine No. 22** *Brading* **with a train for Ventnor. The token exchange is watched by G. H. Gardiner, the Assistant for the Isle of Wight, who can be seen sitting in the signal box.**
G. M. Kichenside

Left: **Bob Church, the regular fireman to Driver Dennis Snow, takes water at Newport to replenish No. 28** *Ashey's* **tanks. Just behind the ladder of the water column can be viewed the "fire-devil" referred to by Dennis Snow in his reminiscences.**
Mike Esau

Members of the Newport Shed Locomotive Department during the 1955 Strike Back row left to right.
Dennis Snow, Ken Simmonds, Sonny 'Ginger' Minter, Manklow, Peter Taplin, Charlie Hackett, John Farrington, Victor Gash, Dick Hollands, Jim Stone.
Middle row left to right.
Jack Nixon, Brian Oatley, Bob Church, Albert Brown, Len Stokes, Sid Stone, Ray Knapp, Tony Tiltman, Ken West, Harold Lacey, Ron Connor.
Front row left to right
Frank Ash, George Ellis, Les Harris, Ted Dale, Ted Joyce, Arthur Turner, Bill Feaver, Maurice Prouten, Bill Reid, Cyril Eason.
Sitting, left to right
Tom Hayward, Ron 'Spud' Hayter.
The Sid Stone Collection

after the sweet tooth of his firemen. When Eddie's mother-in-law arrived on the Island for her annual holiday, 21's footplate crew were always guaranteed bread and butter pudding each day in their lunch box. When Eddie's daughter got married, I had the luck to be working on *Sandown*. We ate wedding cake every day for a month! Driver Prangnell, better known to hundreds of visitors to the Isle of Wight, as 'Uncle Eddie', used to invite tourists up into *Sandown's* cab in return for a donation to the Children's Home at Woking. He must have raised hundreds of pounds for this worthy cause over the years. If one needed help, Eddie was always there – a true friend to all Island railwaymen.

When steam traction ended in December 1966 I stayed on for an extra three months at Ryde depot classified as, 'Driver, put back'. Two O2 tanks were retained to assist with engineering trains for the electrification of the Ryde-Shanklin line, namely Nos 24 *Calbourne* and 31 *Chale*. It therefore fell to me to fire the last steam locomotives for British Railways on the Isle of Wight. What a great pity it is that someone didn't preserve *both*

engines, but thankfully *Calbourne* lives on at Haven Street.

Sid Stone

I guess that if I have any claim to fame on the Isle of Wight railways, it must be as the fireman on the last passenger train from Freshwater. This was a very sad occasion for me and I recall we had No.29 *Alverstone* running bunker first to Newport with just a simple headboard saying, "Last Train". It was the 9.34pm off Freshwater on Sunday 20th September 1953 and crowds turned up to wave farewell.

My family roots came from the Island railways as my father was a fitter at Newport shed and my Uncle Jim was a driver at Newport and later Ryde. It was therefore natural for me to join the railways as a cleaner on 24th January 1947 with the ambition of becoming an engine driver. My regular driver was Ted Dale and later Bill Hayward. We didn't have a regular engine in those days as I was in the lower links. If anything our usual engine would be one of the four Brighton E1 tanks which would pull anything. They were fast on passenger traffic, strong on freight and above all very reliable locomotives. It was possible to forget this power in an E1 at times. I recall being with Driver Bill Hayward on No.1 *Medina* doing some shunting at Newport and we collected two fully loaded milk vans. In those days the milk was carried in metal churns. The E1 tank made light work of these vans and I remember hitting the buffer stops in Freshwater bay platform at Newport. Of course, the milk churns just toppled over and a few thousand gallons of milk ran down the station approach drive.

As if this wasn't bad enough losing all that milk, Bill had a similar experience with me at the Newport paint shops in the old workshops. Arthur Harris, the carriage painter told us to enter the paint shop from the Cowes end with a coach coupled up ready for painting. "We will go in on the handbrake", said Bill. All we had to do was deposit one coach and collect a finished newly painted carriage. As we entered the paint shops we just touched the newly painted carriage and away she went down through the old workshops, knocking over huge pots of paint, and out through the wooden doors at the rear of the paint shops. That sparkling, former Brighton carriage ended up off the rails in the weeds! How Bill talked his way out of that one is another story.

There were some real characters amongst the drivers at Newport shed. Driver Jack Sewell for instance was almost fanatical about keeping his locomotive spotlessly clean – particularly the inside of the cab. I was firing

to Jack one day and noticed that as we were travelling along through the Island countryside he had removed the regulator handle. He then proceeded to clean it whilst the train was in motion. This put the fear of God into me, but the finish on that regulator was just like a mirror!

During the early fifties we had a serious coal shortage on the Island railways and the coalman at Newport, Jim Hewitt was often left with just a few tons of coal on the stage at times. I have even seen Jim's mate 'Nobby' Clarke sweeping the coal stage to gather up

The bird's eye view of Ventnor station seen from the downs above the tunnel, showing a Ryde-bound train pulling away from the unusual arrangement of platforms and adjacent tracks.
R. J. Blenkinsop

Fireman John 'Googie' Withers looks out from the footplate of No. 17 *Seaview* as she heads away from Brading on 10th April 1958, with the 11.42 am Ventnor – Ryde train.

H. P. Mason

dust. Things were so desperate that at times we all wondered if we would be able to run a service.

It was whilst on the Island railways that I had the only major incident of my railway career. We were leaving Freshwater one night on No.29 *Alverstone* and rounded the curve towards Causeway Crossing. Suddenly there was a loud bang and Bill Hayward applied the brake. We discovered that one half of the crossing gates was on our buffer beam. Apparently the crossing keeper (who was a lady) had gone to the pictures for the evening, leaving her father in charge. He had decided to play it safe by leaving one gate open for cars to pass and the other closed while he turned his attention towards a game of cards. Being the first train to pass we of course hit it!

One unusual practice at Newport North signal box, which was situated at the Cowes end of the station, was to collect the Freshwater line single line token hoop on the end of a broomstick! It was a regular occurrence practised by Ron Bennett, Jim Hooper and the other signalman at the box. They would stick the broom out of the signal box window and the fireman of the Freshwater train would just place it on the broomstick. Of course this all had to come to an abrupt end when some-

one took a picture for the local newspaper – The County Press! Where else would one find this sort of activity in everyday use, other than the Isle of Wight railways?

By 1955, the Island railways were gradually being closed, line by line, and it was apparent that with only the Ventnor and Cowes lines open, Newport shed would close. As a 'passed man' at Newport I could see that a move to Ryde shed would result in me being sent back to the ranks of the cleaners. I therefore decided to move to become a driver at Norwood Junction.

John 'Googie' Withers and John Perkis

John 'Googie' Withers

Working on the Island railways literally changed my life and the lives of two of my fellow firemen – John Perkis and John Millward. We all married Island girls who were sisters from the same family and thereby became brothers-in-law, as well as workmates.

I first went over to the Isle of Wight on 3rd March 1947 with no lodgings and nowhere to leave my belongings, at the age of fifteen and a half. A warm greeting awaited me from Driver Harry Peters and his fireman Les King. Les took me home to his mother's house at The Eagle Tavern, and the following night he fixed me up with a bed at his sister's house. My first mate was Driver Fred Hilditch on No.21 *Sandown* as our regular engine until I went into the Army for National Service. When I was demobbed I returned to the Island railways to fire to Driver Harry 'Oh Ah' Linnington on No.21 again.

One early memory of working with Driver Linnington on *Sandown* is of being summoned to Ryde St John's Road by Signalman Dick Russell. Signalman Russell instructed us to proceed light engine, as fast as possible, to Haven Street to assist a failed locomotive on a Medina Wharf-Ryde freight. Upon arrival at Haven Street we were greeted by the sight of 'Ginger' Minter, his fireman, and Cedric Attrill gathering water and pouring it into the tanks of Brighton E1 No.3 *Ryde*, as fast as possible. Apparently what had happened was that Driver Minter's fireman had watered up the wrong locomotive at Newport shed. By shear coincidence Nos 3 *Ryde* and 4 *Wroxall*, both identical black-painted Brighton E1 tank engines had been placed side by side at Newport shed under the ornate water tank. 'Ginger's' young fireman, Dick Morton, had filled *Wroxall's* water tanks to the brim, leaving his own locomotive's water tanks only a third full. My mate, Driver Linnington who was a stickler for rules and regulations never let poor 'Ginger' forget that incident.

From time to time, when the regular engine was in Ryde shed for boiler washout, and it was Driver Linnington's rest day, I had to work on other engines with different drivers. On one occasion I worked on No.14 *Fishbourne* with Driver Jim Hunnybun at the controls. Our turn of duty was to work the 'down' fast to Shanklin, which was non-stop through Sandown. Heading through Sandown station he would instruct me to duck down with him. The station staff and passengers would stare in disbelief looking out for the footplate crew!

One unwritten rule of the Island railways was that you always looked after your fellow railwaymen, wherever possible. In those days a regular good deed went hand in hand with the Mail train duty. After running to Cowes with the Mail train from Ryde, we had to return light engine. Upon heading up the bank out of Whippingham the driver would sound the whistle four or five times. Just past Wootton station we would stop the locomotive and pick up Driver Nelson Parsons.

In 1954 I was passed out to drive in my own right and from then on I was out driving on summer Saturdays or covering for sickness.

John Perkis

Like my brother-in-law John Withers, I too was a fireman on the Island railways. My regular engine was O2 tank No.19 *Osborne* and my regular driver was Arnold Nye. Sadly, No.19 was one of the first three Island O2 tanks to be withdrawn from service, in November 1955 following the closure of some of the Island lines and the subsequent rendering of some locomotives "surplus to requirements". For some time after 19's demise I had to work on No.24 *Calbourne*, which is now preserved at Haven Street in working order. I could never get on with 24 though, as she was a bad steamer in those days and she used an excessive amount of water.

We had lots of tricks to help us in those days as steam engines were extremely hot to work on in the summer months.

John Withers

One of the tricks we used to use in those days as my brother-in-law will recall is that of white-washing the inside of the cab roof. When it was red hot during the months of June, July and August this white-washing would have a nice cooling effect, reflecting the heat. Another trick footplate crews on the Isle of Wight would use during the summer months was to have a swim in the sea whilst waiting at Ryde Pier Head.

Likewise, in the winter we would use the heat from the fire to keep us warm. During the severe winter of 1947 I recall Stan 'Banjo' Jacobs the guard on our train bringing his flask of tea up on to the engine to keep warm at Ryde Pier Head. When we stopped at Sandown Stan walked along the side of the carriage stock to collect his hot tea. Sandown station was in quite an exposed position and snow drifts had blown up along the railway embankments. It was just Guard Jacob's luck to slip into a deep snow drift and be buried for a minute or two! Our next section of the locomotive's working diagram was a trip through the centre of the Island through Merstone to Newport. On arrival at Newport we were greeted by the news that the line was blocked. I asked Wilf Bell, the Newport Station Foreman what we were going to do now, as clearly we would be out all night on No.21 *Sandown*. His reply was something like, "You should have brought your blankets and pillows!"

I often had unpleasant assignments to undertake. One

night duty comes to mind when working a permanent way train at Ryde Esplanade with a colleague, Jim Arnott on engine No.15 *Cowes*. We were waiting for the pw gangers to unload sections of 40ft lengths of track off the bolster wagons. After about half an hour of this rhythmic clanging sound of rails landing on the pier decking, an angry gentleman dressed in his pyjamas came across from one of the Esplanade hotels demanding that we halt our activities immediately!

John Perkis

Working on the Isle of Wight railways on the small O2 and E1 tanks was generally harder than working on the mainland with large Bulleid Pacifics. I can say from first hand experience that this is absolutely true of both types of job. For instance, here is one example that illustrates and supports this statement. On arrival at Ryde Pier Head with a train from Ventnor, Island men had an average just eight minutes to run round a train, couple up, water the locomotive, push the coal forward etc. An equivalent job on the mainland for a Bulleid Pacific would be allowed half an hour. Yes, I can hear you say, but a Bulleid 'West Country' or 'Merchant Navy' Pacific was a much bigger locomotive. True it was. The difference was that mainland crews had ten minutes after completing their work for a cup of tea, but Island crews did not!

John Withers

Mind you there were ways of cutting corners on Island engine duties. One instance comes back to me when working with Driver 'Ginger' Minter on No. 21 *Sandown*. 'Ginger' and I had an agreement that at the end of the day we took it in turns to either clean the ash pan or drop the fire, after running light engine from Ryde Pier Head to Ryde St John's shed. On this particular night upon arrival at Ryde shed it was 'Ginger's' task to clean the ash pan on No. 21, and after screwing down the handbrake I said to 'Ginger', "Good night mate I'm off home now". An astonished 'Ginger' retorted, "Hey Googie, what about cleaning and dropping the fire?" I then had the pleasure of explaining that I had already cleaned out the fire at Ryde Pier Head after filling the boiler up, and that we had run down the pier with no fire!

John Perkis

During steam days if you overslept in the mornings, the Foreman at Ryde shed would send a cleaner around to your house to knock you up. On one such occasion I happened to oversleep and the Foreman duly sent a young cleaner to knock up 'Ollie' Perkis as I was nicknamed. However, by sheer coincidence four doors down the road from me lived an undertaker called, Ollie Perkins. The young cleaner hammered at the door of my neighbour at 4 o'clock in the morning and enquired if I was ready to come to work now. A solemn Mrs Perkins opened the bedroom window and replied, "Young man there are no funerals at this time of the day!'' This completely baffled the young lad.

John Withers

The Island railways had a great community spirit in those days. I remember when I got married all my colleagues from Ryde St John's Road shed came along to see my wife and me off at Brading station. The honeymoon train was pulled by locomotive No. 22 *Brading*, the driver was Alf Goodson and his fireman was Don Pegg. As we departed from Brading the locomotive's wheels went over a series of detonators. At Ryde St John's my regular driver's family arranged to throw rice over us in our compartment. Unfortunately, they chose the wrong carriage compartment and the rice went all over John Perkis and John Millward!

John Perkis

Not long after John's marriage I recall another incident occurred at Ventnor. A new coloured light signal was placed inside Ventnor Tunnel to control access to the platform. Mr Gardiner, the Assistant for the Isle of Wight railways, had travelled down to Ventnor on our train to assess the performance of the new coloured light signals in service. My regular driver was absent from work on this particular day and so I had 'Seagull' Reeves, a 'passed man', with me. After running around our train we ran into the dark smoke filled tunnel. Driver Reeves asked me not to fluster him and let him do the driving, as he was well aware that Mr Gardiner and other bosses were observing the manoeuvre. I told 'Seagull' that it was all right to proceed ahead as the coloured light signal was now green. He opened the regulator and shouted, "O.K. mate don't fluster me". Three or four minutes later we still had not moved out of the tunnel. I therefore decided to speak up, " 'Seagull', sorry to fluster you but did you know we are going backwards towards Wroxall and not forwards into the station!" Talk about a red face!

John Withers

Like my brother-in-law, I had 'Seagull' Reeves as my substitute driver, one night. Now all 'Seagull' was interested in was motorbikes and on this occasion he was praising the capabilities of a particular motorcycle with a colleague. Our guard Stan 'Banjo' Jacobs waved his green flag, blew his whistle and with that Driver Reeves blew *Sandown*'s whistle and opened the regulator. As we set off, 'Seagull' said that he had forgotten to remove a lamp from the front of the engine and instructed me to climb along the side of the locomotive to retrieve it. Passing Ryde Pier signal box slowly, Signalman Vic Hailes shouted out, "Where are you going? You've left your train behind". I passed on this information to Driver Reeves who abruptly came to a halt, and returned red-faced to the platform to couple up.

Footplate crews had to be so observant, particularly on Island lines which were so rural. Entering Brading one day Driver Charlie Humphries thought he spotted a platelayer working on the track so he sounded the whistle several times and applied the brakes. As we approached it became clear that it was actually a horse. Hearing our steam locomotive, the poor horse bolted and we chased the beast all the way into Brading station.

On the Island railways I was always known as 'Googie' Withers, rather than John, having acquired the nickname from the famous film star. Sadly, the time came for me to move off the Isle of Wight to Fratton depot for promotion as a driver.

John Perkis

Like my brother-in-law, I also moved to Fratton for promotion, in February 1960. It was sad for all the family to see the Island railway network gradually being closed line by line to its present truncated form. Who knows, perhaps one day the Isle of Wight Steam Railway from Wootton to Haven Street will join up again with the BR line at Smallbrook, then the fun will start!

Fred Janaway

I came across to the Isle of Wight following my redundancy from St Leonards in 1947. Here I was engaged on firing a variety of Eastern Section locomotives such as 'Schools' class, L1 4-4-0s Wainwright C class 0-6-0s and various interesting engines of Brighton pedigree. From February 1947 I joined Driver Tom Hayward on the Ventnor West branch working on the Brighton "Terrier" tanks Nos 8 *Freshwater* and 13 *Carisbrooke*. After a spell of National Service in the Army, I returned to find two different engines carrying the same nameplates working on the Ventnor West branch. The "Terrier" tanks had been returned to Eastleigh for future work on the Hayling Island branch and had now been replaced by two O2 tanks Nos 35 *Freshwater* and 36 *Carisbrooke*. Both locomotives were painted in lined black, fitted with Island style extended coal bunkers and motor train equipment fitted for push-pull train working.

After about twelve months of working with Driver Fred Harvey on the push and pull service, between Merstone and Ventnor West, the authorities realised that my seniority of service meant I should have been in the top link at Newport shed. I was therefore quickly reallocated to work with Driver Dick Hollands on No. 34 *Newport*. The trouble with Dick was that he was too good an engineman and never wished to open No. 34 up. This caused me problems with fire and gave me a lot of hard work. Nevertheless, Dick was a great friend and tutor as well as a real character with his cigarette holder and obsession for lubricating the motion and parts of *Newport*. This enthusiasm for oiling even went to draining off so called empty cans in order to use their contents in his own supply!

The beauty of having a policy of footplate crews having a regular locomotive, instead of a common user system was that drivers tended to treat their allocated engine as personal property and therefore give it extra care and attention. It was a real 'family atmosphere' on the Island and I had an added advantage in being able to lodge with my uncle, Jim Hewitt, the Newport shed coalman. This had its advantages of course in that my engine often had prize, 'pick of the bunch' special lumps of coal supplied by Uncle Jim!

One Boxing Day Uncle Jim offered to coal up my O2 tank and make sure she was ready for her turn of duty. In return Uncle Jim asked for a ride on the footplate down to Ventnor. When I arrived on shed, I peered into 34's coal bunker to find it over-flowing with choice best coal. Furthermore, Uncle Jim had placed so much coal in the firebox, that I had little to do in the way of firing for most of the first hour or two of duty – other than use the dart to liven the fire up!

During the summer service, Newport shed was given a triangular diagram turn of duty. The duty commenced with a trip from Cowes to Ventnor working chimney first. The second section of this Saturday duty was to return to Ryde Pier Head bunker first, concluding with a final working chimney first towards Newport and Cowes. This resulted in the locomotive facing in the opposite direction to which it started at the end of its turn of duty. Now Newport shed based engines facing chimney first towards Ryde, whereas Ryde St John's Road shed locomotives faced bunker first towards Ryde Pier Head. At the end of the triangular Saturday turn of duty, the Newport based engine was therefore required to work "backwards" until it worked the Saturday tri-angular turn the following week. This was very confusing for drivers who halted their engines in station platforms because Newport based drivers were accustomed to looking out for painted platform markers indicating where to stop. As the locomotive was now working backwards with the driving position on the opposite side, they were now working blind. I experienced this problem with Driver Dick Hollands on *Newport* one week. Dick relied on my help and guidance throughout the week as to where to halt the engine for water etc. He did attempt to help himself when halting trains at stations by finding new temporary stopping marks. At one such Island station Dick selected to halt No. 34 in line with a row of carrots planted in Bill Shiner's garden. This worked well until one day Bill Shiner dug up his carrots!

When diagrammed to work from Cowes to Ryde we would take water for the engine at the column situated at the end of the platform under the footbridge. Likewise, water would be taken when working from Ryde to Cowes from the "balloon" column situated at the end of the platform at the Cowes end of the station. As often as not we would regularly have Harold Blundy as our guard for the train. This fine gentleman took a real pride

O2 tank No. 29 *Alverstone* passes over the Medina drawbridge in Newport station with a train for Cowes. Waiting in the 'up' platform is another O2 tank ready to depart for Ryde as soon as the line is clear. *R. J. Blenkinsop*

in appearance with polished buttons and flower in lapel – a credit to the Island railway staff. It was Harold's custom that while we were taking water on the engine, to make his way over the footbridge and drink a quick cup of tea in the refreshment room. This worked out well when working trains to Ryde and even better with trains working to Cowes, as the guard's compartment in the brake carriage would be right outside the refreshment room on the Cowes platform. In the summer this was all very well as there were five or even six coach trains. Guard Blundy had to be somewhat quicker on his feet during the winter timetable season as trains were shorter, being of three or even two coaches in length. Finally, one day it had to happen that Harold was caught out. We had a two-coach train and Harold forgot that his guard's compartment was positioned next to the engine. He waved his green flag from outside the refreshment room as normal, but realised too late what he had done! Oh dear, poor Harold's face was a picture.

On another occasion I found myself in trouble with Mr Bell who was in charge at Newport, following an incident that was no fault of my own. I was waiting to leave Newport station with a train for Freshwater. I turned on the Westinghouse brake pump known to all railwaymen as the donkey pump. As I turned on the donkey pump a jet of water shot out containing all sorts of filth and oil. Unfortunately, at that precise moment two well dressed ladies were waiting parallel to the apparatus, and were splashed by the pump's discharge! The ladies took exception to this and made an official complaint to Mr Bell. The boss then instructed me to make out a full report of the incident. My reply went something like this, "Mr Bell, I wish to relate, before proceeding with the 4–8, I put on the donkey pump and water came out, and two old ladies started to shout. It was purely an accident. It wasn't a sin, that their cheap summer dresses now looked like leopard skin!". Upon receiving this poetical reply he was not amused.

Now two of our Newport engines used to have minds of their own, Nos 25 and 33. At the time both engines were fitted with Drummond design boilers and when the brakes were applied the injectors came on for some reason. This could be very dangerous if the injectors came on during a token exchange with a signalman, as it was possible for the poor man to be scalded by boiling water!

When the new guard's hats came out I noticed that they had a strip of gold braid on the peak. Not to be out-done I duly attached a strip of brass to my cap through the kind help of the Newport signalman. Now as it happened I was on relief turn for Driver Bill Bishop on No. 29 *Alverstone*. This engine was polished to perfection by her fireman, Ken West. This young lad was as keen as mustard and after doing some shunting in the yards, young Ken returned to his spit and polish on his side of the cab. The time came to collect my transformed driver's hat – complete with brass braid strip from the Newport signalman. As we passed by the signal box on the engine, he held it out for me to collect. However, I forgot that the door was open and promptly fell off the footplate of the locomotive. Meanwhile young

Looking through the fireman's spectacle on No. 14 *Fishbourne* as it sets off down Ryde Pier with Driver 'Ginger' Minter at the regulator on 5th August 1966.

G. S. Cocks

"Westie" carried on polishing oblivious of what had happened. Eventually he had the good sense to apply the brakes. What made it worse was that it happened at the time the film the "Titfield Thunderbolt" was being screened locally and I ended up getting a bit of a leg pull. Nevertheless I continued to make sure I was one of the best dressed enginemen on the Island complete with flower in button hole, when possible!

Sadly, I had to leave the Island for promotion, but I am very fortunate in having a set of former Island railwaymen as colleagues with me at Littlehampton where I still work today.

Don Saunders

I was demobbed from the RAF in March 1947, having come home from Gold Coast in West Africa, which is now known as Ghana. For the first five or six weeks after arriving back in England, I went to my wife's home in Darlington. I then received a letter from my father on the Isle of Wight informing me that there was a cottage available for us at Ryde, if we cared to move down. After a few days in Ryde, I applied to Reg Megget, the Loco Superintendent for employment as an engine cleaner. At first he informed me that he was unable to take on cleaners over the age of twenty-one, but he asked my date of birth again and said I could start at 8 am on 19th May 1947.

On the Wednesday morning, my third day on the railway, I was told by Chaddy Willis that I was to relieve the night cleaner and that this would be my first firing turn. It was with some trepidation that I stepped onto the footplate of an 'up' train at 8.15pm to be confronted by the somewhat imposing figure of Driver Jack 'Jumbo' Elliot. As we left the station bound for Ryde Pier Head he turned to me and said, "I haven't seen you before". "No Sir," I replied, "I only started on Monday". His next question was, "Have you just come out of the forces?" "Yes Sir, the RAF", I told him. Driver Elliott retorted, "Well never mind. I expect we will manage as long as one of us has our feet on the ground!" At first I took this to be pure sarcasm, but was to learn that it was typical of the dry humour of the most even-tempered and equable natured men I have ever met in my life. This humour was to be demonstrated to me again in a short time. Having arrived at Ryde Pier Head, I was shown how to uncouple the brake hoses and lift and stow the engine coupling. Then the reverse procedure after we had run around the train. Jack Elliot made the fire up at the same time while we stood in Ryde Pier Head platforms, explaining the principles of firing a steam locomotive, after which, Driver Elliot made me practice working the injector to fill the boiler.

Upon leaving Ryde Pier Head it was the practice not to fire before leaving Ryde Esplanade Tunnel, and often not before leaving Ryde St John's Road. He had me pull the fire through with the pricker as we came out of the tunnel and that was all. When we left St John's Road, Driver Elliot pointed out the bright spots and told me to fire to them. The shovel had a long narrow blade, and as our coal that day was pure dust, I picked up a miniature Mount Everest and swung it towards the fire door as Jack opened the door for me. Unfortunately, the footplate of moving trains are not steady surfaces and I suddenly lurched forward so that the edge of the shovel blade was heading straight for my driver's leg. Stopping the shovel before it penetrated the flesh to the bone was easy enough, but stopping its load of dust was altogether different. This slid off to the end of the blade and completely ran over Jack's ankle and foot. I remained in my bent over position and waited for the storm to break. He looked down at the coal, then at the firehole and finally at me "If you had told me you were going to do that," he said, "I would have gone outside for awhile". Nothing further was said about this matter but the sequel came some ten months or a year later. Driver Elliot's regular fireman was a 'passed man' and he was booked to do a driving turn, hence I was instructed to cover for him for the day. Jack arrived for work carrying both his lunch box and a large bag which

he kept carefully folded over at the top. Once again we relieved on our way up to Ryde Pier Head, but later, on our way to Ventnor, we stopped at Ryde St John's Road station. Here Jack sat down, removed his shoes, took a pair of Wellington boots from the large bag and carefully put them on.

"The Lord helps those who help themselves", he said. "Blessed be the name of the Lord."

As a 'passed cleaner' I fired when required to every driver in Ryde Depot and to 'passed firemen' as well, so gained the experience required. It must be remembered that the O2 class engines had been designed to haul 100 ton trains, but on the Isle of Wight in the summer months these small tank engines were pulling sets of six coaches on the Ryde – Ventnor line of 150 tons unladen! Consequently water was the big problem and anything less than a full head of steam resulted in a rough trip.

My regular driver was Jack Bradford who came on loan for the summer from Barnstaple. We were in the 'Brading Harbour gang' on the Brading to Bembridge branch of $2\frac{1}{4}$ miles and one chain, although we did other work as well. One Sunday morning we ran light from Brading to Bembridge to pick up the two coach set. Our guard, who shall remain nameless, had not worked on the Bembridge branch for some years. Upon arrival at Brading we went onto the branch then onto the train, where it was my job to couple up. The signalman then gave Driver Bradford the 'single engine in steam key', which entitled us to work on the branch and was necessary at Bembridge. Upon arrival at Bembridge, while I uncoupled the engine from the coach set, the guard collected the key from the driver and then walked up into the signal box. There wasn't enough room for a pair of points at Bembridge in order for the locomotive to run around the train, and so the engine was taken back onto a turntable and turned about an eighth of a turn onto the run-round road. Meanwhile the guard had used the key to unlock the master-lever which he then pulled to release the lever frame. Next, he pulled a second lever to unlock the points at the Brading end of the run-round loop and finally a third lever which moved the points over and also closed the catch points half way along the run-round road. On this occasion he pulled the first two levers correctly but made a mistake with the third and merely unlocked the coal siding points. Having pulled his three levers he waved a green flag out of the signal box window and Jack Bradford set off with the engine, while I walked along the platform ready to couple up again. The guard, not sure if Jack had seen the flag, ran down the steps and put his head out of a window. Seeing him appear, Jack immediately applied the brake, only to see the green flag waved again. This actually distracted Jack from looking at the catch points and so he threw the regulator open again and promptly became derailed with the wheels on one side sinking into a freshly dug allotment.

The engine finished up leaning over on its side and we therefore had to send for the breakdown gang from Ryde. As Jack considered that the guard was too shocked to be trusted he said that he would throw out the fire from the engine. Meanwhile, I was to walk down the track, carry out the protection rules and meet the breakdown train. I therefore started to plod my way along the sleepers and place one detonator at a quarter of a mile, one at half a mile and three ten yards apart at three quarters of a mile as the rules required and proceed to meet the breakdown train. When it arrived I climbed up onto the footplate and explained to Mr Megget, the Loco Superintendent, the situation as I had last seen it. We then approached my three detonators, but ran over six! Then two more detonators and finally another two! Mr Megget asked me "What game was I playing?" I told him I had only booked five detonators. The truth was almost unbelievable. While Jack was busy throwing out the fire on the engine, the guard had walked along the track and considered my detonators to be five yards out in each case, and had placed his own charges on the line. He had then gone through the fence onto the Toll Road, flagged down a bus and had a free ride back to Bembridge.

My next regular driver was O.P. Vallender or, 'Rabbits' as he was known to the railwaymen on the Island. It was he who taught me most about steam engines on No. 24 *Calbourne*. It was a most enjoyable time as he was a very good driver to work with. Then the youngsters who returned from National Service came back to Ryde depot. This meant that I had to return to the ranks of the cleaners as they were senior in service to me, although I still had regular firing turns. It was during this period that another amusing episode happened to me.

We had a driver whose name was Lord Charles Humphries. He was one of three brothers who had been given Lord, Duke and Earl as Christian names. Lord Charles was called Lord by his wife, but was better known to us as 'Clinker'. Owing to some minor health problem he was transferred into the Brading Harbour link. His regular fireman didn't hit it off with 'Clinker', and consequently was not very interested in the job. He was therefore a poor fireman and there was an unpleasant atmosphere on the footplate. I was sent as a replacement fireman when his own mate had two weeks annual leave. I make no claim to have been a better fireman than anyone else, but throughout the two weeks I was constantly being told what a wonderful fellow I was. It was my practice to always have a 'large bottle' on the footplate and drink it as required. Generally I would drink at least three bottles of water per shift. 'Clinker' brought a bottle of concentrated orange juice and insisted upon adding it as required to my drinking water.

So we came to the last trip from Bembridge with Driver 'Clinker' Humphries on the final Saturday of the two weeks. Having turned the engine, I mounted the platform to pay a visit to the gents. Upon returning to the footplate, 'Clinker' then told me what a pleasure it had been to have me firing for him over the fortnight, and insisted upon me accepting a packet of twenty Craven A cigarettes, which I detested but were his favourite brand. Then the guard gave the 'right away' and set off. Upon glancing back I noticed that 'Clinker' had forgotten to couple up the carriages whilst I was

in the gents as they were now stationary at least fifty yards behind us! I shouted to 'Clinker' and he heaved the reversing lever over and we shot back onto the train, where I coupled up and away we went again. 'Clinker' then told me what a totally useless object I was and that his own regular mate was a miracle worker compared with me! My future as a railwayman was doomed to failure. Furthermore he wanted his cigarettes back and I owed him about half-a-crown for all the orange juice I had consumed; I gave him both his cigarettes, which had been mine for all of four or five minutes, and also a half-a-crown. However, I must confess that I was laughing so much that it hurt. It wasn't the incident itself, but it was the fuss after the totally unwarranted compliments he had been heaping upon me. In the words of King David, "How the mighty are fallen!" From idol to ashes in five minutes!

My next regular driver was Roy 'Ricky' Rodwell and this too was a very enjoyable period. He was also the first driver to let me do some of the driving, on No. 35 *Freshwater*, so I did one trip out of the three, which constituted a normal shift diagram.

I was moved yet again and became the regular mate to Bill Vallender known as 'High Dry' on No. 17 *Seaview*, to replace his regular mate Peter Harbour. Bill was a cousin of my earlier driver, O.P. 'Rabbits' Vallender. Upon Bill's retirement I became regular driver to 'Ginger' Minter. It was with 'Ginger' that we hit the herd of steers as mentioned by 'Ginger' in *Once Upon a Line Volume One*, which incidently happened on 28th December 1961, not 1962.

In 1959, I passed for driving and so became a 'passed fireman'. My first driving turn was to work a fireworks special from Cowes to St John's Road, then to Ventnor after Cowes Carnival. My fireman was a cleaner doing his first firing turn.

We took over at Ryde shed when it came out of service and cleaned the fire etc. I oiled round and backed the loco up for coaling. Another engine backed down in front of us and I told them that we were due to move off. They informed me that they would move out of our way as soon as they had 'squared up!' On returning to the footplate of my engine I looked into the sandboxes and found them empty, and so told my fireman to fill them up while I went and made the tea. He came in after a while and told me it was all done. We then picked up our train, ran empty to Cowes, loaded up our passengers and set off for Ryde. All was well until we were approaching Newport when it started to pour with rain. Leaving Newport and climbing through the short tunnel up Fairlee Bank the wheels began to slip. Nothing would stop them until finally I had come to a complete stand. Upon examination, I discovered that the sandboxes were as empty as they had been in the depot. Despite the evidence the fireman swore by all that was holy that he had filled them completely. I therefore sent him to walk back to Newport for assistance from the second fireworks special, which incidently was being driven by my regular driver, 'Ginger' Minter. He duly came up behind with his O2 tank and banked us away.

Upon arrival at Ryde St John's Road, while I ran

Above: **Ryde shed cleaners. Left to right Dan Wheeler, Des Gallop and Doug Saunders, standing on the front buffer beam of No. 21 *Sandown*.** *John Withers*

around the train and filled up with water, my fireman and a cleaner ran to and from the shed with buckets of sand to fill her up and rectify our deficiency. The rest of our journey to Ventnor was trouble free, but I was sent for the following day and given a dressing down by Mr Bob Menzies, the Loco Foreman. I was told in

the process that not only was it my job to instruct my fireman, but to ensure these tasks were carried out. The mystery was not resolved until some days later, when several of us were sitting in the lobby and the remark was made that the young cleaner/fireman I had out with me was going to make an excellent railwayman, as he was so keen. In view of my experience with this same lad, my opinion was somewhat different. I was then reminded of that firework's night when the locomotive in front had backed down. Having moved back for coal, my fireman had come back and filled their sandboxes for them! Although I informed Mr Menzies of this and it caused him to laugh, he said that it further demonstrated the need to check in future. It just wasn't my day.

In May 1962 I transferred to Slade Green in Kent as a driver on electric stock. In October 1965, I became a 'relief' Motive Power Foreman at the same depot, and

Below: **Driver Roy Rodwell gently applies the Westinghouse brakes on No. 35 *Freshwater* as she approaches Ryde Esplanade station on 10th July 1965. There is evidence that Firemen Ray Lewns has been hard at work as the safety valves are just lifting. Further up the pier a Cowes train can be seen waiting to depart from Ryde Pier Head station, while behind the station canopy can be observed the chimney of the paddle steamer *Ryde*. Approaching the Pier Head from the left is one of the Sealink motor vessel ferries. The photograph is full of detail which will bring back memories to many Isle of Wight railway enthusiasts.**
Tony Scarsbrook

in September 1974 I became Train Crew Supervisor, still at Slade Green, but I look back to my days on the Isle of Wight as the best training possible for my present job.

Ray Lewns

I'm not a Southern Railway man by birth as I was born in the very heart of Great Western country at Bristol, close to the sound of locomotives with copper capped chimneys and brass safety valve covers. It wasn't until 1937 that we moved to Ventnor. After leaving the Army in 1948 I joined the railway as a cleaner at Ryde shed on 31st May of that year. Here I stayed working my way up the ladder to a passed fireman before steam finished. To begin with I just fired on odd occasions or during the summer season, one of which was spent on No. 19 *Osborne* firing to Driver Harry Linnington. Two further summers were spent with Driver Jim Stone firing on No. 25 *Godshill.* Eventually, I became the regular fireman to Driver Roy Rodwell on No. 35 *Freshwater* and this was my main job from 1959 until 1966. As a 'passed man' during the summer season, I was given my own engine to drive and someone was sent out to fire for me.

One early memory of Ryde shed concerns the E4 0-6-2 No. 2510 which was sent over on a trial basis to answer the need for a more powerful locomotive to work trains on the Ryde – Ventnor section. Sadly, Ryde crews didn't really have an opportunity to get to know the new locomotive as the E4 had clearance difficulties on the curved platform at Ryde Esplanade and likewise to a lesser degree at Ventnor. I recall her last appearance at Ryde shed when it was sent to Newport shed. The return diagram to Newport was the night freight. Driver Mike Tucker climbed up into the cab to take over the controls and I remember asking Mike, "How did he go about starting her off?" His cryptic reply came back, "Never mind starting, how do you stop her?"

Sometimes it was possible to swap shifts with other firemen and in so doing we experienced working on different engines with different drivers. On one such occasion I worked on No. 14 *Fishbourne* with Driver 'Ginger' Minter. He was a really super driver who was willing to teach one the craft of being an engineman, as I was to discover. 'Ginger' turned and offered me the opportunity to drive No. 14 with a fast train from Ryde Pier Head to Sandown and I readily accepted and gave Driver Minter my shovel. As we passed through Ryde Esplanade Tunnel, 'Ginger' said, "We've got a good fire, open the big valve and let her go". With this knowledge I readily obliged, and old *Fishbourne* began to throw out black clouds of smoke over the six carriages behind us. We made it to Sandown with time to spare, but on the return journey passing through St John's Road we spotted some chicken houses on fire. At the pier, we were greeted by Driver Bill Vallender who informed us that our engine exhaust had caused the fires!

Another change of duty turn took me on No. 21 *Sandown* with Driver Harry Linnington. It was the height of the summer service and at such times all Island engines needed to be at their best to cope with the heavy six-coach Ventnor trains. On this occasion, the coal supplied was horrible dust mixed with briquettes which was just compacted coal dust in the shape of an egg. With this quality of coal, I therefore had to build up a big fire in 21's box. We set off light engine to Ryde Pier Head station where we coupled up to our six-coach train, and with time to spare I decided to eat my sandwiches. A few minutes later I noticed a man wandering around our engine giving it some close inspection. Driver Linnington stretched out of his right hand side of the cab and enquired if he could be of any assistance. Back came the reply "I am Inspector Bolland" and with that he climbed up onto the footplate. Quite briskly, Mr Bolland opened the firebox doors and peered inside. His next comment really set the cab of No. 21 alight, "Fireman, you've got more than your regulation nine inches

Having run around its train at Ventnor, No. 20 *Shanklin* creeps up slowly onto the end of the coach set. Evidently Ray Lewns, who is pictured looking out from the footplate, has his regular engine in at Ryde shed for boiler washout as *Shanklin* was the spare engine.
Courtesy of Ron Brett

Above: **Driver Frank Ash and Fireman Terry Hatcher's Drummond boilered No. 18** *Ningwood* **approaches Truckles Road bridge, between Smallbrook Junction and Brading, with the 11.25 am Ryde – Ventnor train.** *H. P. Mason*

Below: **This picture is a fitting tribute to the enginemanship of Driver Frank Ash and Fireman Terry Hatcher as they pound up Apse Bank aboard their regular engine, No. 18** *Ningwood* **with a Ventnor-bound train on 19th June 1965.** *Tony Scarsbrook*

of fire". With this Driver Linnington became incensed, "What! What did you say? Get your coat off and catch hold of that shovel and try working with nine inches of fire with this 'excuse' for coal to Shanklin, let alone Ventnor. If you can keep steam up to normal with half a gauge glass of water I will be happy!" Immediately, the good inspector decided to beat a hasty retreat and was not seen on the Island for some time after.

When one did have a bad fire there were ways of retrieving the situation. One day when on my regular engine No. 35 *Freshwater*, we were supplied with some diabolical coal. The dust was irritating my skin and burning my neck when mixed with the sweat. Every trick and dodge was tried to get a good fire going – all to no avail. Passing through St John's Road I could see we were in for a rough trip as the fire was turning black. We struggled on past Smallbrook and began to experience some difficulty in getting the injector on to provide water in the boiler. I turned to my driver, Ricky Rodwell, and asked him what we should do. By this time we were going down hill under Wall Lane bridge on the approach to Brading. "Watch this," he said, and with 75% cut off he opened the regulator as wide as possible. Next, Driver Rodwell dropped the reversing lever out. This had the effect of sharpening the blast from the chimney as we were in full forward gear. As if by magic, before we entered Brading 35's fire was really glowing and brought back to life.

The worst few weeks I ever experienced with Ricky Rodwell on *Freshwater* had nothing to do with the engine's performance however. The time I refer to was the dreadful winter of 1962/63. Waiting at Ryde Pier Head one morning, I remember Shunter Jim Yeo pointing out ice flows from *Fishbourne* and a frozen sea shore at Ryde. What a contrast I thought to the sunshine Island with its beaches packed with swimmers. The paddle steamers were experiencing problems and trains were at times delayed. On one very cold day during three trips to Ventnor I had to wear my reefer coat to keep warm, almost unheard of with the usual warm glow from a firebox.

Only once while out driving an engine have I experienced a real problem. It was a weekday, during the summer service, with a six-coach train to Ventnor that a nightmare became reality. Starting off from Ryde Pier we experienced continual difficulties with getting the injectors on engine No. 17 *Seaview* to function correctly. The locomotive behaved like a pig starting off from Shanklin and I wondered if we would get up Apse Bank. Upon reaching Wroxall the lead fusible boiler plug blew, and immediately my fireman set about blackening down No. 17's fire before any more damage was caused. Using ballast from beneath the track we quickly achieved this. It wasn't long before Ryde shed sent some assistance to pull the train into Ventnor and get the dead *Seaview* back to the depot for repairs and inspection of the damage. Not long passed before I was sent for to appear before an inquiry into the incident, but before I left fellow drivers led by Ted Dale presented me with a pile of fitters' defect cards for No. 17. Boilersmith Joe Snellgrove informed me of his findings. He had discovered that the water could not enter *Seaview's* boiler as the clack, which forced water into the boiler, was almost seized up with limescale. This failure of injectors had been reported by Driver Dale and his colleagues. At the Inquiry I produced my evidence, and immediately the case was dismissed.

On returning to Ryde shed I was greeted by my old friend Passed Fireman 'Lester' Stan Piggott. He informed me that he had just hit and killed a farmer's prize bull as he passed through the bridge at Wootton on his way to Haven Street. The bull had ventured onto the line, and O2 tank No. 31 *Chale* hit the bull with the bunker first position – leaving Stan virtually no chance of spotting the beast in the pitch black darkness until it was too late. After making an official report about the incident, his colleagues, including myself, thought we would have some fun. We asked Stan if he was going to turn up to work in the morning and tell his regular driver, Harry 'Toby' Watson JP about the incident on the footplate, or at his Magistrates' Court in the afternoon!

All of us who worked on the footplate on the Island railways have some rich memories and one of my favourites is the time we were outside Wroxall with the mail train to Ventnor. Just before Wroxall station the home signal was sited next to the bacon factory and as we approached on No. 35 *Freshwater* the red signal remained down. Driver Rodwell blew 35's whistle several times and eventually sent me ahead to see the porter-signalman. As I approached the platform, along trotted a semi-dressed Signalman Harold Unstead who had overslept. With the signal still set against us, Harold invited us to continue our journey with the main train with these words, "Come on in nipper – get going, the road is set for you. Never you mind the signals."

So it was with great sadness that on 31st December 1966 I had to say farewell to my friends like Signalman Unstead and my loyal footplate companion on *Freshwater* Driver Roy 'Ricky' Rodwell. My last Island turn of duty was the morning shift on No. 14 *Fishbourne*. We gave her everything on the way back for the shift change and as I climbed down from my faithful loco I had to come to terms that it was transfer to the mainland for work on electric trains.

Andy Fryer and Terry Hatcher

Andy Fryer

I worked on the Island railways for nine years from 1958 until the end of the steam era, starting at Ryde St John's Road as a cleaner. As a fireman my regular engine was the Drummond boilered No. 31 *Chale* with Driver Cyril Eason at the regulator. She was a super engine and one of only two of our O2s fitted with Drummond boilers – the other being No. 22 *Brading*. The Drummond boilered engines differed in appearance to their Adams boilered counterparts with dome top lock up safety valves and a whistle instead of a hooter. The former Newport drivers who came to Ryde when their shed closed in 1957 seemed to get on well with the two Drummond boilered engines. When they 'notched-up' on the

Right: **Footplate friends Driver Frank Ash, left with Fireman Terry Hatcher right, aboard their regular engine, No. 18 *Ningwood*.**
Courtesy of Mrs June Ash

Below: **O2 Tank No. 18 *Ningwood* has just arrived at Newport with a freight train from Medina Wharf. The train crew obligingly pose for the camera. Left to right Fireman Terry Hatcher, Driver Frank Ash and Guard Jack Tharme.**
Tim R. Genower

reversing lever, drivers Cyril Eason or his opposite turn driver, Denny Snow, would use a bolt and go up one and a half notches instead of two. It was therefore an easier task to work as a fireman when these drivers adopted this technique. If we had a fully loaded six-coach train climbing up from Shanklin on Apse Bank, Cyril would notch-up two and a half giving just a touch of second valve.

A common complaint from Ryde drivers, who preferred the Adams boilered O2 tanks, was that Nos 22 and 31 were erratic steamers and would prime frequently. Not so – nothing could be further from the truth. The secret when firing these two engines was to keep the water level in the boiler down and avoid this unnecessary priming. They would steam easier and had more power than the Adams boilered types.

Lunchtime outside Ryde St John's Road shed on 21st February 1966, Left to right Fireman Andy Fryer, Driver Maurice Prouten and Fireman Terry Hatcher.

Terry Hatcher Collection

Terry Hatcher

I joined the railways in late 1951 at Newport and worked on all the Island lines with the exception of the Brading – Bembridge branch. My regular engine on which I fired was No. 18 *Ningwood* which was driven by Frank Ash. She was generally a good engine but on one occasion we did encounter problems with the Westinghouse brakes in the midst of Ventnor Tunnel. After leaving Wroxall, with a fully loaded six-coach train we began to slow up more than usual on the 1 in 88 gradient on the approach to the tunnel. As *Ningwood* entered the inky, black depths speed dropped dramatically resulting in us coming to a dead stop. Frank then asked me to climb down and pull all the brake cords underneath the carriages. It was a job to breath in this steam and smoke filled confine and by the time I returned to the footplate I was gasping for air. Driver Ash then was able to continue using the handbrake only to stop us. Such was my christening on becoming a fireman.

Like Andy Fryer on No. 31 *Chale* my engine, *Ningwood,* had a Drummond boiler for many years and it was only in the latter years that it was reboiled with an Adams type. I can certainly whole-heartedly support Andy in his argument that the Drummond boilered O2s had far better steaming qualities and power than their Adams boilered counterparts.

One day, I recall a nasty incident on No. 18 when approaching Shanklin. We were drawing into the platform when suddenly there was a loud bang. Being frightened I climbed off the footplate, but Driver Ash, quite calm and collected, reassured me that things were under control. "Shut the cylinder cocks nipper, it's only the gauge glass that has broken" shouted Frank. He was truly master of his engine.

Andy Fryer

My favourite route to work on was the Cowes – Newport – Ryde line and I used to spend much time at Medina Wharf, which was located on the 'up' side of the single line between Newport and Cowes. Although coal traffic remained to the end, the sidings were sadly overgrown and neglected in those last few years. Even after the closure of the Cowes line for passenger traffic, the Wharf remained in use for off-loading of rails to be used for the electrification of the Ryde – Shanklin line.

Terry Hatcher

I recall one unfortunate incident I was involved in at Medina Wharf. We were shunting wagons with No. 18 *Ningwood,* into the Quay road siding, ready for coal to be loaded from coal boats tied alongside the Wharf. After completing this work Frank Ash drove No. 18 up to the top half of the yard, where our guard, Roy Phythian, was sorting out various rakes of wagons to be made up into a forty-wagon train for Newport. Roy asked us to push eight wagons back into number five siding, but before they passed over the point, the blades of the point sprang back. The eight wagons then took the wrong line and began to pick up speed down the gradient towards the weighbridge. Frank blew *Ningwood's* whistle several times to warn anyone at the bottom of the gradient. Roy Phythian, Frank and myself just had to stand and watch those wagons make their way to the stop blocks which they completely knocked down, sending a cloud of coal dust high up into the air. No one was to blame as the points were faulty.

On another occasion we were on a Cowes – Ryde train with *Ningwood* when we were halted at Smallbrook Junction outer home signal for some minutes. Frank sent me up to see what was the reason for our delay. Before I could get to the box, Signalman Vic Hailes greeted me and explained that there had been an earth slip on an embankment just ahead of us causing an obstruction. The alert Vic Hailes had saved us from certain derailment and injury to ourselves. His prompt actions certainly deserved a medal, but perhaps mention here will be some recompense.

Andy Fryer

I had a scare one morning on No. 22 *Brading* when coming through Ventnor Tunnel. At the time, I was just a young fireman with little experience of Driver 'Mad' Jack Sturgess. As we came out of the tunnel mouth, bunker first towards Wroxall, I looked across the cab to ask Jack if we were going back to shed after arrival at Ryde Pier Head, but there was no sign of the driver! I couldn't believe it, my driver had completely vanished. Had Jack fallen off the footplate of 22? Should I stop the train or continue to Wroxall and summon assistance. I walked across the footplate and took control of the regulator. Looking through the cab window spectacle on the other side of the glass was the smiling face of Driver Sturgess. Knowing that I was a young fresh lad, he had climbed out of the cab and scrambled along the frames to hide whilst we were still inside the tunnel!

Terry Hatcher

The worst winter I ever had to work through while in service on the Island railways, was that of 1962/63. On the night of the blizzard that froze everything up and literally paralysed the Island railway network, Driver Frank Ash and myself were asked to put away seven engines at Ryde St John's shed. The Shed Foreman said, "Book what you like Frank. We are desperate!". Frank cleaned out the smokeboxes of all the locomotives while I cleared the fires. After coaling up the engines in preparation for the next day we backed as many O2 tanks as possible under the cover of the shed buildings or just at the side of the building out of the biting easterly wind. Eventually we finished work at about 2.30am but had to walk home to Newport.

Andy Fryer

When I woke up to go to work the morning after the blizzard, all I could see was a white landscape, snow everywhere. Living in Cowes, how was I going to get to Ryde shed for work? I walked down to Mill Hill station to discuss the situation with Porter Horace Cade. Telephone instructions came through from Ryde to "stay

In winter hibernation at Sandown, awaiting the return of the tourists for the summer season are locomotives Nos 27 *Merstone*, 16 *Ventnor*, 32 *Bonchurch* and 18 *Ningwood*. Note engines 27 and 18 have Drummond boilers.

H. P. Mason

put" and help out at Mill Hill. There were several of us and we were all given shovels and sent to walk along the line towards Newport to clear any drifts of snow covering the track. Some hours later we had managed to walk as far as Cement Mills Cutting. Here we discovered an O2 tank embedded in a wall of snow. Peter Mills was at the regulator, but the wheels and side rods were buried in the snow and the engine could not move. Eventually a second locomotive arrived to assist and they pulled the whole train out of the drift.

Terry Hatcher

Shortly after the thaw, No. 18 *Ningwood* happened to fall into the hands of another driver. Frank really looked after *Ningwood* in order to ensure that she was in first class working order. On this occasion, Frank observed Driver Harry Watson really going all out up the pier where we were waiting to take over the controls for a train to Ventnor. When Frank climbed onto the footplate he really gave Driver Watson a tongue lashing. With this Harry argued that *Ningwood* was not the personal property of Driver Frank Ash. Frank however pointed out that he looked after the engine and had just packed her glands. This demonstrated to me what a conscientious driver Frank was, and just how much the policy of regular engines paid off as any criticism against your engine was taken personally.

Andy Fryer

Not so much care and attention was lavished on the spare engines at Ryde shed. We were given these locomotives to use when our regular engines were in for boiler wash out or overhaul. Drivers didn't care how much these locomotives were flogged. From 1958 until their withdrawal the spare engines were Nos 16 *Ventnor*, 20 *Shanklin*, 25 *Godshill*, 26 *Whitwell*, 30 *Shorwell*, and 32

Above: **Driver 'Ginger' Minter waits impatiently on Sandown platform and looks to see who are the crew on the approaching train from Shanklin. Fireman Andy Fryer looks on from the footplate of No. 14 Fishbourne.**
Mike Esau

Left: **Passed Man Ray 'Joe' Maxfield prepares to take water on No. 17 Seaview at Ryde Pier Head on 7th August 1965. Back on the footplate Fireman Andy Fryer is busy at work with the shovel building up a good head of steam before setting off for Newport.**
Tony Scarsbrook

O2 tank No. 17 *Seaview* simmers in the Freshwater bay platform at Newport station, with Fireman Andy Fryer chatting to Passed Man Ray Maxfield who is out of view on the other side of the cab. Meanwhile, Harry Ridgeway is busy supervising the loading of mail bags into a PMV on 7th August 1965.

Tony Scarsbrook

Bonchurch. The latter engine, No. 32, was a particularly poor steamer. During the winter months this motley collection of engines would be taken down to Sandown for storage. Here their cabs would be boarded up, chimneys covered and all parts heavily greased. Just before the summer season timetable came into operation, as often as not it would be my task to travel down to Sandown and prepare them. After removing all wooden boards from the cabs and chimneys, I then had to degrease them. This task usually took about four hours, leaving me the afternoon free to watch the trains go by!

Roger 'Chalky' White

By the time I joined the Island railways in March 1961 all we had left was the Ryde – Cowes and Ryde – Ventnor lines and our locomotive stud consisted entirely of

O2 tanks. Promotion to fireman in 1963 came quickly and I joined Driver Eddie Prangnell on engine No. 21 *Sandown*. Of course many of my reminiscences are already recorded in *Once Upon a Line Volume One* and I can verify that all that Driver Eddie Prangnell mentions is 100% true!

Something Eddie forgot to mention was the time we did a spot of fly shunting with No. 21 *Sandown* in Ryde 'down' siding with a three-coach set. We uncoupled the stock from 21 and Driver Prangnell climbed up into the guard's compartment of the brake coach. Meanwhile I opened *Sandown's* regulator and fly shunted the three-coach set into the 'down' loop. Unbeknown to us, there were some visiting British Railway's Southern Region officials from Wimbledon on the Island and they just happened to be on Ryde St John's Road 'down' loop platform. The distinguished gathering watched the three-coach set approach the platform where they stopped and out climbed Eddie. They were so amazed the officials were literally dumbfounded and said not a word!

An amusing incident happened to us on the Cowes line one day. We were heading on No. 21 *Sandown* from Haven Street to Wootton. Towards the end of the long straight when rounding the curve into Wootton, we

Above: **Passed Man Joe Maxfield, pictured looking out of the fireman's left-hand side of the footplate of No. 17 *Seaview,* has handed over the controls to Fireman Andy Fryer. They are backing up to couple onto a carriage set, but note the artful Harry Ridgeway has cadged a ride on the locomotive's steps.**

Tony Scarsbrook

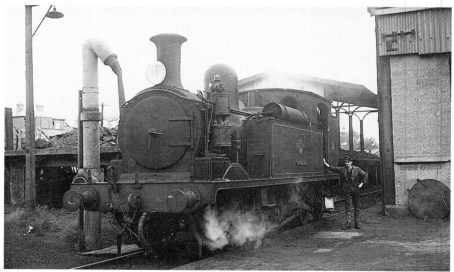

Right: **Fireman Roger White stands beside spare engine No. 16 *Ventnor* outside Ryde shed on 21st May 1964, having given Dr Hendry and his son Robert a footplate ride.**

Dr R. Preston Hendry

Above: **Drummond boilered O2 tank No. 31** *Chale* **enters Brading with a train for Ventnor. The trackbed of the line to Bembridge can be seen behind the locomotive.**

G. M. Kichenside

Left: **Driver Pete Harbour (left) and Fireman Roger White with No. 21** *Sandown* **at Ventnor.**

Roger White Collection

spotted a pheasant on a sleeper, which had apparently been knocked over and was down. "We'll have that on the way back," shouted Eddie across the cab. Sure enough on our return journey Driver Prangnell applied the Westinghouse brake on No. 21 for me to climb down onto the bottom step of the cab. As we approached at about 10 mph I reached forward to scoop up the bird, making sure to hold onto the engine's hand rail with my other hand. Suddenly, the pheasant loomed up but I caught it and took it back onto the footplate for Eddie's dinner.

Driver Eddie Prangnell took the words of the hymn, "All things bright and beautiful" quite literally and *Sandown's* cab was polished to perfection. Her brass work glistened and had a mirror finish. However, in 1964 she went into Ryde Works for major repairs. Following her return to service, Eddie and I set about restoring the brass work to its former glory. A few weeks passed and 21 failed us out on the Ventnor road resulting in a return to Ryde Works. Again, after *Sandown's* return to traffic, I set about polishing the brass work and green copper pipes. Sadly, it wasn't long before the old girl had to return to the Works again for more repairs. This time when the locomotive returned to the shed I rebelled and refused to clean up the brass work. Eddie and I compromised and I agreed to clean the cab while Driver Prangnell concentrated on the brass work; a real spit and polish effort.

Driver Eddie Prangnell frightening the life out of someone, as usual.

The Church of England always seemed to produce railway enthusiasts from amongst its clergy – the late Bishop Eric Treacy and Reverend W. Awdry of "Thomas the Tank Engine" fame come to mind. This railway enthusiast trend was also true on the Isle of Wight, and my local vicar, the late Reverend John Shaw of Holy Trinity in Ryde, was keen on obtaining a footplate ride aboard an Island O2 tank. I therefore asked Eddie for

permission to give the vicar a footplate ride twixt Ryde and Ventnor. The Rev. Shaw arrived at St John 's Road complete with dog collar, overcoat and beret and we climbed up onto the footplate of No. 21 *Sandown*. To our surprise, Eddie discovered that he already knew the vicar, and it wasn't long before the Reverend Shaw was offered the regulator of 21. From then on the vicar regularly joined us for trips to Cowes and Ventnor, when his pastoral duties permitted.

On odd occasions I worked on other engines with different drivers. An incident comes to mind, which with hindsight is amusing, but at the time was quite horrendous. I was sent out to fire for Driver Ted Dale and we were working a Cowes – Newport – Ryde train. Working with Ted Dale was always an enjoyable experience and after taking water at Newport it was non-stop running bunker first all the way to Haven Street with four green coaches behind us. Upon arrival at Haven Street, Signalman Hughie White strolled up the island platform ramp and asked for the single line token for Newport to Haven Street as normal. We searched high and low for it in the cab. What had happened was that the porter at Newport station had obtained its release from the token machine on Newport platform from Signalman Ron Bennett in Newport 'A' signal box. He had then accidently left it on top of the remote control token machine expecting us to collect it. Unfortunately, at the time we were both involved in engine requirements. The Haven Street signalman, Hughie White, therefore got on the internal telephone to his Newport colleague, Ron Bennett and with some very discreet, well chosen words they released the next service train from Ryde to run through the Haven Street – Newport section without its token. No one was ever the wiser and not a word was said!

That was the spirit I will always remember about the Island railways – everyone helping each other. After leaving the Isle of Wight in August 1966 for promotion to driver at Epsom, I eventually transferred to Littlehampton. Here I joined some distinguished former Island railwaymen, namely Fred Janaway, Arthur Budden and Don Pegg.

Johnnie Howe

The first few weeks of the summer timetable in 1964 were a bit of a nightmare for Island footplate crews and shed fitters alike. Unfortunately with so many of the engines requiring major attention in the workshops at Ryde during the winter, the necessary maintenance programme had not been completed. I recall that I was fireman to Driver Maurice Prouten and we had changed engines for the third time on one day. With all the problems we had encountered, I forgot to take water at Ryde St John's Road. Our train was bound for Ventnor. Before we reached Wroxall on the climb up Apse Bank the water situation became rather critical and Driver Prouten decided to uncouple at Wroxall in order to go ahead light engine to Ventnor. After replenishing our side tanks at Ventnor we returned to Wroxall to complete the trip. The next day Maurice Prouten received a letter asking

With just eleven engines in serviceable condition, emergency coaling facilities are laid on at Ventnor to cut down on coaling up at Ryde St John's shed. No. 29 *Alverstone* waits to depart with the 13.20 to Ryde while No.26 *Whitwell* is serviced over the pit on 11th July 1964. In the foreground Foreman Bill Smith discusses arrangements with Ventnor Signalman Syd Sartin, while the fireman of *Alverstone* is standing on the bunker, arranging the loco coal and shouting instructions to Jack Collard. Note the emergency coaling crane.

John Goss

why we had delayed the boat train in the return direction!

In order to work the summer Saturday service, fourteen locomotives were required to be turned out in full working order. By 1964, there were sixteen O2 tanks left with No. 32 *Bonchurch* withdrawn awaiting scrapping alongside St John's Road shed. In theory this gave us two spare engines. In fact for two weekends in July 1964 the Island railway authorities maintained the summer service by hiring a road crane and placing it at Ventnor to coal engines from adjoining coal wagons. By so doing, returning to Ryde shed for coaling and servicing was cut out.

Going back to my early days as a cleaner at Ryde St John's shed, on the night shift one evening I recall having to abandon work owing to heavy rain. In fact, we had

been suffering from appalling Atlantic gales for the two previous days. Two other cleaners, Joe Maxfield and Joe Moore, accompanied me along the track to check the tunnel and general condition of the permanent way. We discovered that the water level was up to the tops of our Wellington boots, but a train service was just about possible. The three of us then decided to return back into the dry at St John's Road shed for a cup of tea. Presently, a driver came in and asked us what the black shining objects were further up the yard. The two Joes volunteered to set off and investigate, but soon returned very excitedly saying the river had burst the wall further up the yard and a flash flood of water was cascading down towards the station, signal box and sheds. Joe Maxfield explained that the black shining 'stuff' was the blowers from the smokeboxes floating on the water. Within minutes there was four feet of water flooding the track, resulting in the cancellation of trains. How lucky we were not to have been swept off our feet and drowned whilst walking the track just minutes earlier.

It was a well known fact that at Ryde shed drivers would change their overalls to oil up their locomotives. Inevitably, some of the cleaners would skip cleaning under engines where it did not show and therefore upset many drivers. One day, unknown to me, Driver Alf Goodson's engine, No. 22 *Brading* was in for boiler

Opposite page top: **No. 26 *Whitwell* with Fireman Johnnie Howe leaning out, ready to collect the token, approaching Smallbrook Junction with a morning train to Ventnor on 7th August 1965.**

Tony Scarsbrook

Opposite page bottom: **Fireman Johnnie Howe hands the single line token for the Haven Street – Smallbrook section to Signalman Vic Hailes as he passes by on O2 tank No. 30 *Shorwell*, bound for Ryde.**

G. M. Kichenside

Right: **Driver Harry 'Toby' Watson JP and Fireman Johnnie Howe (left) pictured at Newport station on 8th October 1965 on board No. 21 *Sandown*.**

G. H. King

Below: **The summer Saturday non-stop fast train 'zooms' through Brading from Ryde, headed by No. 18 *Ningwood*. Signalman Roy Way prepares to collect the single line token from Fireman Dave White, closely watched by Tom Becky.**

Mike Esau

The hand of Fireman Dave White is seen directing the peep pipe onto the coal in order to spray water thereon, thus keeping the dust down on No. 30 *Shorwell*, prior to leaving Mill Hill with the 10.30 train for Cowes on 6th September 1964.
John Goss

washout and I was instructed to clean her. With oily cotton waste I set about giving the engine a thorough clean from top to bottom. Whilst I was cleaning underneath right back around the webs, I heard something clink in the inspection pit below me. I assumed it must be one of the ring nuts holding the cork for oiling had come off. When I had finished cleaning, I climbed down and searched around the floor of the pit for the nut, but instead I found a half a crown which I carefully placed in my breast pocket of my overalls. The following day when we were having our tea, Driver Goodson, who had a reputation of bad temper, came into the cleaner's room and enquired who had cleaned his beloved No. 22 *Brading*. No one answered and all eyes came my way, so I asked Alf if it had been the engine that had been in for washout. His stern reply was "yes", and then a grin appeared on his face. "Did you find your reward then nipper? That's the only bet I didn't mind loosing," and with these words he left the room. The other cleaners peered at me bemused. Apparently, Driver Goodson had said to some of his fellow drivers that he was on a good safe bet and would never lose his money.

When I became a fireman my regular driver was Doug Saunders on No. 17 *Seaview* and many happy unforgettable hours were spent twixt Ryde, Cowes and Ventnor. If you didn't do your job right with the O2 tanks there was little power in reserve, which differed immensely from those crews who worked on the crack expresses on the remainder of the Southern Region, driving their 'Merchant Navy' Pacific locomotives with their tremendous power output.

Ray Harvey

I guess that I hold the record for the shortest period of railway service on the Isle of Wight railways – just two and a half days! I started work at Ryde St John's Road shed on a Monday morning at 8 am, but finished my railway career on the Wednesday at mid-day. Apparently I was hired after a medical from the railway doctor at Shanklin had passed me as medically fit, but when

Above: **Coalman Jim Hewitt (left) is pictured in action shovelling coal from the Ryde St John's shed coal stage into the bunker of O2 tank No. 27 *Merstone*. Meanwhile, *Merstone's* fireman is selecting some large choice lumps of coal for his fire.**
Rod Hoyle

Left: **O2 tank No. 30 *Shorwell* rounds the curve from Newport Tunnel with a train for Newport and Cowes.**
David Benning

my medical report reached the Waterloo Office they discovered that I had a defective left eye, so they ordered me to stop work immediately. I was heartbroken as I left Ryde shed and many a tear was shed as I walked up to the Labour Exchange. However, I did have two and a half a days of cleaning and riding on the O2 tanks up and down the shed roads, and was able to watch my engine driver heroes at work at close quarters.

When Driver 'Mad' Jack Sturgess retired we became good friends and as a small consolation he gave me his Southern Railway guard's whistle which he used to scare lurking passengers, as described on page 87 of *Once Upon a Line Volume One*. The incident that I will always remember involving Driver Sturgess occurred at Haven Street station, when Jack was approaching the station with a train from Ryde. The train from Newport had just arrived in the station, but the Ryde inner home signal was in the 'on' position against Driver Sturgess.

However, Jack was an impatient man and decided to "jump the signal", as he saw the line ahead into Haven Street was clear. This 'Mad' Jack did, but the Porter Signalman at Haven Street ran out of his signal box to give Jack a good mouth full! To prove that the incident actually happened I recorded it on film. In later years Jack calmed down but we often talked about life on the Island railways. Yes, I will treasure for ever the memory of those two and half days of work at Ryde shed. How lucky were the men who worked on the railways for a longer period of time!

Heading out of Newport station over the Medina drawbridge with a train for Haven Street, Ashey and Ryde. This photograph is now an historical record in itself as both the viaducts carrying the line to Ryde (left) and the line to Sandown (right) have now been demolished to make way for a modern dual carriageway road.
R. J. Blenkinsop

Right: Isle of Wight Central Railway 4-4-0 tank No. 6 under the locomotive hoist at Newport, receiving attention from the fitters. According to the late Bill Miller this engine was renowned for 'hunting' in a side-to-side movement. This gave the permanent way staff additional problems as this, combined with its weight, tended to damage the track.
Dr J. Mackett Collection

Below: The staff of Newport Works, Isle of Wight Central Railway stand for the camera in front of a Brighton "Terrier".
Dr John Mackett Collection

Above: **Members of Newport locomotive shed staff during the 1925 Strike.**
Left to right - Back row: Jim O'Dell, Les Stocks, Fred Payne, Bill Bishop, Laughton, unknown, Bert Morris, George Prouten.
Middle row: Percy Rogers, Charles Morris, unknown, Tommy Stanbury, unknown, Fred Ray, Alf Ainsworth, Harold Lacey, unknown,
Arthur Wiltshire.
Front row: Lu Hogfish, Ted Dale, Jack Sewell, Reg Southwell, Bill Harms, Harris, Ted Joyce, P. Watson.

The Lintern Family Collection

Below: **Fireman George Ellis (left) with Driver Chiverton on the footplate of Brighton "Terrier" No. 10 *Cowes* outside Newport shed.**
The Ellis Family Collection

Above: Beyer Peacock 2-4-0 tank *Ryde,* pictured outside Ryde shed in April 1934. This locomotive had been withdrawn two years before this picture was taken and during this period of time had been stored under cover at the back of Ryde shed. Her last duties prior to withdrawal were on the Bembridge branch. Much effort was made to preserve this engine on the Isle of Wight through the offices of Mr Stretton-Ward. Eventually *Ryde* was transferred to Eastleigh to join other candidates for possible preservation, but when war broke out, she was unfortunately broken up in August 1940.

Pictured in front of *Ryde* are left to right Shed Driver Alec Russell, Signalman Bob Lambert, Coalman Sam Wells, Porter George Jenvey, Albert Brading, Painter Mickey Rodwell, Guard Stan Jackman and Shed Fitter Harry Cull.

Dr John Mackett Collection

Below: **A Newport shed crew on a Ryde engine! Left Fireman Harold Lacey. Right Driver Jim Bannister.**   *George H. Hunt*

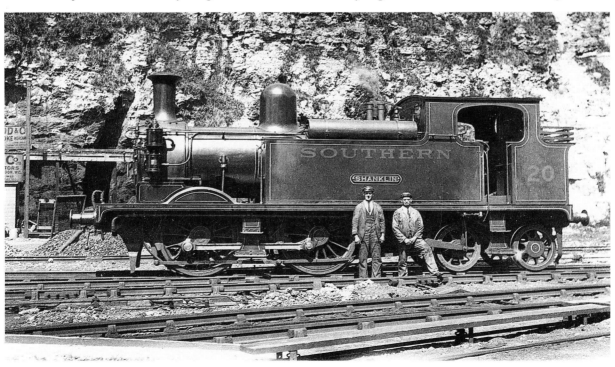

Left: **Remembrance Day at St Lawrence station. The train crew, pictured left to right, Guard Stan Jackman, Driver Ernie Chiverton and Fireman George Ellis, pause to reflect and remember lost friends and colleagues who were killed in action.**
The Ellis Family Collection

Below: **No. 22** *Brading* **looking immaculate in her pre-war Southern olive green livery at Ventnor. Left Passed Fireman Eddie Morely. Right Driver Fred Cass.**
George H. Hunt

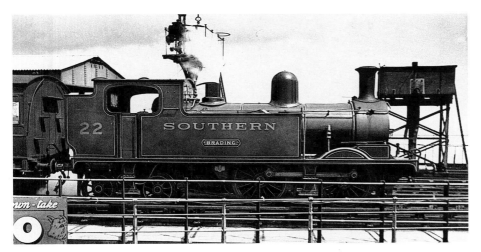

Left: **Polished to perfection, pride of Ryde shed, No. 22 *Brading* seen here at Ryde Pier Head complete with Driver 'Mad' Jack Sturgess on the footplate. The only things missing are flowers on the front buffer beam bracket!**

J. R. G. Griffiths

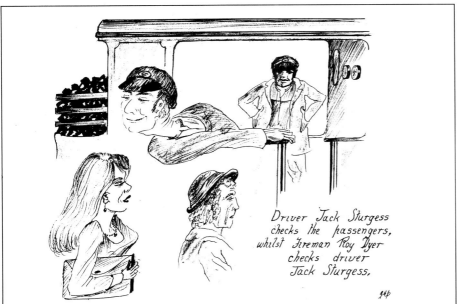

Driver Jack Sturgess checks the passengers, whilst Fireman Roy Dyer checks driver Jack Sturgess.

Below: **No. 28 *Ashey* has just uncoupled ready to run around its train at Sandown, prior to returning to Newport and Cowes. The number board 15 indicates the duty number.**

J. R. G. Griffiths

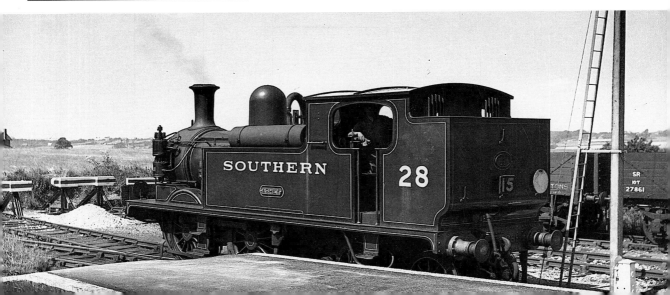

Above: **Fireman Dave Rendell, known to Island railway staff as 'Jed Clampett', replenishes the tanks of No. 20 *Shanklin* at Ventnor, whilst Driver Stan 'Lester' Piggott looks on. The Downs formed an excellent backcloth for this photograph which was taken on 19th February 1966.**

G. S. Cocks

Left: **Left, Driver 'Ginger' Minter and Fireman Ray Hobden wait at Shanklin aboard No. 14 *Fishbourne* ready to depart with an afternoon train for Ryde on 5th August 1966.**

G. S. Cocks

Below: **Left, Fireman Tony Toogood. Right, Driver 'Mad' Jack Sturgess.**
Courtesy of Mrs P. A. Bartlett/Sturgess Family Collection

Above: **How to make a token exchange when you already have a train on one platform – Isle of Wight style! Fireman John Hix makes the token exchange with Signalman Dick Randall at Wroxall on 7th August, 1965. Looking through the spectacle of No. 21** *Sandown* **can be seen Driver Ted Joyce.**

Tony Scarsbrook

Left: **Left Fireman Bob Church. Right Driver Bill Hayward on No. 33** *Bembridge* **at Ventnor.**

David Benning

Above: **Driver Jim Hunnybun is giving No. 14 *Fishbourne* full regulator and Driver Roy Dyer adds to the smoke effects on No. 27 *Merstone* as they race past towards Smallbrook on the 07.40. train to Ventnor on 13th June 1964. Both locomotives are fitted with Westinghouse pump shields to prevent oil from splashing onto passengers and adjacent coaching stock when working bunker first. This idea of pump guards was disliked by footplate crews and by the end of 1964 they were nearly all removed from Island engines.**

John Goss

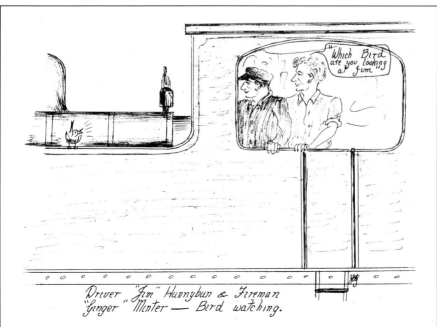

Driver "Jim" Hunnybun & Fireman "Ginger" Minter — Bird watching.

"Which Bird are you looking at Jim"

Left: **Inside Ryde shed are Nos 21** *Sandown* **and 15** *Cowes* **with Fitter's mate Major Coombes and Cleaner R. Withers looking out from 21's cab.**

Ronald J. Post

Below: **Ryde St John's Road shed was always a popular place to visit for railway enthusiasts in steam days. After arriving on the Portsmouth – Ryde ferry, Andrew Britton (left) and Timothy Webb have made the shed their first destination. They are pictured in front of No. 31** *Chale* **which will later take them down to Ventnor.**

John A. Britton

Newport Driver "Ted Joyce" very anxious to commence his Duties.

Below: **Brighton E1 tank No. 4** *Wroxall* **with rear driving wheels removed under the hoist sheer legs at Ryde Works on 4th August 1959. This was the last time a locomotive of this class received mechanical attention as this last survivor was withdrawn from service in October 1960.**

H. P. Mason

Right: **This late afternoon photograph taken at Ryde shed reveals that the steam age was not all glamour and romance, for at the end of the day the fireman was still required to clean the fire out and empty the smokebox. No. 35** *Freshwater* **has just arrived back on shed after a hard day at work, hauling trains to Cowes and Ventnor. She is pictured waiting on the pit ready for Fireman Ray Lewns to get to work.**

John A. Britton

Below: **The Ryde Works wheel tyre lathe in May 1962. This essential piece of machinery was installed in 1874 and was originally powered via an overhead steam driven line shafting. In 1913 it was converted to electric motor drive. A crane was also installed to work with this apparatus in 1924, in order to remove the faceplates, toolposts and head and tail stocks. During the steam era Ryde Works apprentices ran a competition involving the wheel tyre lathe to see who could turn the longest wheel shaving waste when a locomotive's wheel was turned during tyre reprofiling. The record is held by former Ryde Works Chargehand Bill Smith, who unrolled his metal shaving from the Works to Ryde St John's signal box!**

H. P. Mason

The bogie wheels from No. 27 *Merstone* come off the wheel turning lathe at Ryde Works, following a tyre reprofile. Pictured left to right are Les Coote, Bert Jackson, Peter Malone, Bob Pope and Bert Presswell.

Dr John Mackett

Right: **The Kirstall Forge 2 ton hand crane No. 425S photographed outside Ryde Works in 1962. The crane had a massive octagonal section jib adorned at the head and foot by some artistic castings. The crane was often used by works staff on very unofficial activities, such as to assist with scrumping from a neighbouring orchard!**

H. P. Mason

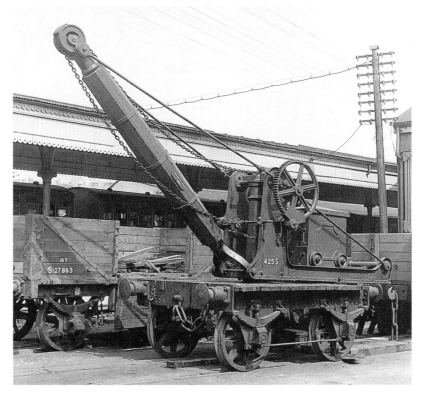

Below: **Driver Frank Ash's regular engine, No. 18 *Ningwood* receives a major overhaul in Ryde Works in May 1962. The overhaul included replacing her Drummond boiler with a reconditioned Adams boiler. The replaced Drummond boiler later reappeared on No. 31 *Chale* in January 1963.**

H. P. Mason

Above: **No. 29** *Alverstone* **with Driver Ted Dale at the controls on the 10.18 am Ryde – Cowes service approaching Smallbrook Junction on the cold snowy morning of 28th December 1962.**
H. P. Mason

BOILERSMITHS CALENDER

Joe Snellgrove from Ryde Works, was an expert with a Hammer by day, & a lawn Mower at Week ends.—

Below: **Snow on the Sunshine Island! Driver Jim Stone accelerates past Smallbrook Junction on No. 25 *Godshill* with the 11.25 am, Ryde Pier Head – Ventnor train on 28th December 1962.**

H. P. Mason

Left: **A privileged group of enthusiasts are given special permission to clean the locomotives rostered to haul the LCGB "Vectis Farewell Special". Pictured in the midst of cleaning No. 24** *Calbourne* **at Ryde St John's Road shed are left to right Steven Cole, Richard Lightbown (on the boiler), Adrian Searle, Derek Gawn and Philip Hayward (on the steps). Apparently the photographer, Tony Bennett, regularly organised volunteer cleaners to prepare the engines for the summer Saturday double-headed trains.**

A. E. Bennett

Below: **Driver John Townsend gives the single line token to Signalman Vic Hailes at Smallbrook Junction as he passes on a Cowes – Ryde service train on 10th July 1965.**

Tony Scarsbrook

Above: **O2 class tanks Nos 14 *Fishbourne* and 24 *Calbourne* with the LCGB "Vectis Fare- well" rail tour train at San- down on 3rd October 1965. Both engines have a good head of steam as their safety valves have lifted.**

G. S. Cocks

Right: **All out assault on Apse Bank as Nos 24 *Calbourne* and 14 *Fishbourne* are both on full regulator, the sound of which was greatly appreciated by pas- sengers and line-side enthusiasts. Great compliments were paid to drivers West and Bradford for their outstanding climb of Apse Bank on this LCGB Special.**

John Goss

Above: **No. 24** *Calbourne* (pilot engine) and **No. 14** *Fishbourne* (train engine) pause at Wroxall for a photographic stop whilst en route to Ventnor. Both drivers, Jack Bradford and Ken West are enjoying a quick cup of tea on engine 14 but Fireman Terry Drudge has wandered back along the ballast to see how long they will be before departing.

Timothy P. Cooper

Four stalwarts from Ryde Works — from left to right Foreman Albert Brading — Sub Foreman Harry Fullwood — Carpenter George Mears & Blacksmith Alf Rees, engaged in a very serious consultation.

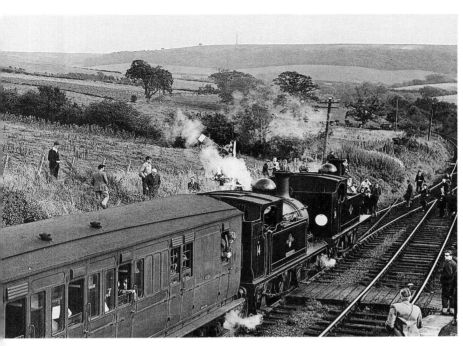

Above: **The signal is pulled off ready for departure from Wroxall and both footplate crews have returned to their respective locomotives.**

G. S. Cocks

Below: **Fireman Tony Toogood takes water on No. 24 *Calbourne* as No. 14 *Fishbourne* waits its turn after the arrival of the LCGB "Vectis Farewell" Special at Ventnor.**

G. S. Cocks

Above: **A unique sight at Ventnor – a double-headed train on the LCGB Special headed by Nos 14** *Fishbourne* **and 24** *Calbourne,* **while on the right is a normal service train headed by No. 28** *Ashey.* **The three are photographed by hundreds of enthusiasts.**

G. S. Cocks

Below: **Driver Jack Bradford eases the regulator open as No. 14** *Fishbourne* **runs back onto the LCGB "Vectis Farewell" train after running round at Ventnor.**

G. S. Cocks

The final weeks of steam on the Isle of Wight are typified by this picture as an engine was attached to either end of the train between Ryde St John's Road and Ryde Esplanade.   *R. J. Blenkinsop*

Memories of the last steam hauled train on 31st December 1966
by Peter Harbour and Ray Knapp

Peter Harbour

As luck would have it, I was given the last driving turn on a steam-hauled passenger train on the Isle of Wight. This turned out to be the 9.40 pm to Shanklin from Ryde Esplanade which returned to St John's Road. Our engine was the oldest O2 tank then in existence, No. 14 *Fishbourne* built in 1889. As so often happens, the boat connection from Portsmouth to Ryde Pier Head was late in arriving and we eventually left about twenty minutes late. On the footplate with Ray Knapp my fireman, and myself were Alderman Mark Woodnutt the Island MP, a BBC radio sound recordist, Mr Davis the Ryde Loco Foreman and another young chap whose name escapes me. Behind the engine we had a train packed with five hundred passengers festooned with tape recorders, cameras and flags.

At each station large crowds turned out to cheer, and

along the route car horns were sounded. After uncoupling the engine on the rear of the train at St John's Road, I opened up the regulator on No. 14. This resulted in the old girl priming and losing her feet a bit, but this was controlled and we got away to Smallbrook briskly. As we headed through Whitefield Woods the Island MP Mark Woodnutt passed a flask of whisky around the footplate. Now as a rule I never drink alcohol whilst on duty, but on this occasion I decided to accept the offer and had a swig. From Truckells Bridge I punched the regulator to give *Fishbourne* a burst up to the summit and then eased off down into Brading, my home town. After the right away from our guard, Roy Yule, I opened the regulator and No. 14 slipped in full gear, but immediately notched up and we built up speed past the chalk siding. Heading over Morton Common we must have been doing close on 40 mph with a nice bark coming from 14's Drummond chimney. As we entered Sandown station there were loud cheers and flashes from the cameras of waiting photographers.

The start away from Sandown was against the loco on the gradient, but *Fishbourne* gave her very best with a full load behind. It was just like an 'old summer Saturday' loading resulting in a lot of fireworks from the chimney as sparks and red hot cinders cascaded over Los Altos Park. From Lake Bridge, No. 14 was going all out and it seemed unreal that this was the very last trip to Shanklin this engine would undertake. Arrival at Shanklin station was a sight I will never forget with hundreds of cheering people gathered on the platforms. After running around the carriages with the loco, I made my way up into the signal box for a chat with Signalman Ted Johnson.

Ray Knapp

When Pete arrived back from the signal box, I had to request our footplate visitors to leave us for a few minutes while I built up the fire for the return journey. On the way down it was impossible to do much with the crowd on board, so at Shanklin I made sure that we had a full head of steam for the return journey. After doing this I climbed down from the footplate with about sixty detonators which I had taken from the engines stabled at St John's Road shed. I placed these along the line out of Shanklin as far as I could go in the time. Then I ran back to the engine and gave some last minute

attention to the fire using the dart and shovelled on the last few shovel fulls of coal before starting off.

Peter Harbour

We were now ready for the return trip to Ryde and after the "right away" we used 14's whistle almost continuously as we passed over Ray's detonators, thus assuring a spectacular departure for steam from Shanklin. Mark Woodnutt brought out the whisky flask again which was passed around those present on the footplate. Now the police left Shanklin when we departed and they followed our passage along the line stopping at every bridge to Ryde. What they were expecting I don't know.

Ray Knapp

Heading through Whitefield Woods I shouted across to Peter, "At least we haven't had the communication cord pulled".

Peter Harbour

Ray's words were prophetic for from Smallbrook we must have had the cord pulled at least six times!

Left Alderman Mark Woodnutt MP. Centre Fireman Ray Knapp. Right Driver Peter Harbour. *Richard Stone*

Above: **The final hours of steam at Shanklin, 31st December 1966.**

136

Below: **Scenes of the last steam hauled passenger train 31st December 1966. Left Fireman Ray Knapp. Right Driver Peter Harbour.**

G. S. Cocks

Richard Stone

Ray Knapp

We eventually arrived at St John's Road with just 80 lb of pressure, little fire and hardly any water in the boiler, we just about made it into the shed. The remaining engines were there, but they were cold, quiet and waiting in lines with no future work to do – not even a wisp of steam or a hiss from a pipe could be heard. It was a ghostly situation and not a pleasant sight when one thought about the fate awaiting those Island stalwarts.

Peter Harbour

The whole yard was dark and deserted and there was just one light on in the shed. While Ray dropped the fire and cleared up, I removed the wreath which had been placed on 14's bunker. Quickly and quietly I placed this into my car boot as my memento of that last trip, and then returned to say my farewells. It was a peculiar, almost eerie atmosphere as Ray and I looked over Ryde yard across the condemned engines. We said goodbye to each other as Ray had to leave the Island for a mainland job, like so many others or be made redundant. Our shift which had started at 2 pm now finished and we made our way off 14's footplate and out of the shed. It was a sad farewell to those glorious years of steam.

The end is near. No. 31 *Chale* in a partial state of dismantling in Ryde Goods Yard on 29th August 1967. The scrapping of this locomotive was temporarily halted by Kings of Norwich in view of a preservation attempt. Alas it failed, but there could so easily have been *two* O2 tank engines preserved if only someone could have found just £800.
G. S. Cocks

Chapter Two – Stories from the Guards

Wally Thrower and Jack Tharme

Wally Thrower

Originally I came to the Isle of Wight on a Territorial Army exercise and whilst in Sandown I met my wife. After getting married I joined the railway in April 1956. At first I worked at Ryde Pier Head as a temporary porter for the summer season and eventually was made permanent. From being a humble porter I went on to learn how to drive the auto trucks and tram cars. At a later date, I transferred to Ryde St John's Road as a senior porter which in reality turned out to be the duties of the booking clerk. At first I found this job quite interesting, but after a change of staff in the offices I decided to leave to become a goods guard.

Jack Tharme

I started some time before Wally in April 1943, and like Wally I thoroughly enjoyed my time working as a goods guard. In steam days everyone used to 'muck in' and help each other on various jobs. Quite often we have had to cope with a wagon or two off the rails in Medina Wharf. Now instead of calling out a breakdown gang from Ryde we set to and rectified the situation ourselves, ie – driver, fireman and me the guard. On one occasion Driver Harry Peters was taken ill whilst driving his locomotive, No. 20 *Shanklin* on a Ryde-Ventnor train. Rather than stopping everything his fireman drove the engine while I fired all the way to Ventnor! Meanwhile,

Miss Elizabeth Winter and Guard Jack Tharme pose next to No. 22 *Brading*, which has just been attached to a special train at Ryde St John's Road on the last day of steam traction, 31st December 1966.
G. S. Cocks

Driver Peters "recovered" back in a first class compartment on the train. Where else would this sort of practice have gone on?

On another occasion Driver Ted Dale forgot to collect the single line token when leaving Newport. Luckily I spotted the mistake and collected it from the signalman as we accelerated from the platform. Meanwhile, Ted chuffed away merrily on No. 29 *Alverstone*, all the way to Haven Street, where he spotted his mistake. By this time I had managed to clamber along the side of the carriage on the running board and hand over the missing item to his fireman, before entering Haven Street.

When mishaps did happen on the Island railways we would always try to laugh them off. I remember being involved in an unfortunate incident at Ryde St John's Road. Early one morning I came to work and as usual I wandered over to Ryde Works to ask for any spare scrap wood for lighting a fire in the staff rest room, but on this occasion they could not help. I therefore abandoned this task as time was short and set to work shunting at St John's Road Yard. Driver Alf Goodson on engine No. 22 *Brading* opened up the regulator of his O2 tank and loose shunted some loaded coal wagons. Fine, we thought, as they gathered speed down the siding but we suddenly spotted a freshly painted carriage straight out of Ryde Works stabled just in front of the stop blocks. Those loaded coal wagons hit the carriage which went up and over the stop blocks and down on top of one of Ryde Works' wooden storage sheds. Well, I was 'volunteered' to go across to the Works to report the incident. I knocked on the office door and told Bill Smith the following, "You know you said you didn't have any scrap wood. Take a look out there, Bill!" His reply is unprintable needless to say.

Wally Thrower

I also had a lot of fun as a guard and I particularly enjoyed working back the last passenger train at night from Ventnor. This return working was always guaranteed to be a fast run to St John's Road. On one particular night we left Ventnor with two bogie vans and engine No. 18 *Ningwood* driven by Frank Ash. The practice at Wroxall was to run straight through and hand out the token to the waiting signalman. As we passed through Wroxall non-stop Driver Ash handed out the token to Signalman Unstead and then fully opened up the regulator on old No. 18. We roared down Apse Bank, but came to a sudden halt just outside Shanklin at the home signal. Waiting for us was Signalman Ted Johnson who informed Frank that Signalman Unstead at Wroxall had not received the token. After some searching round we discovered the loop and pouch single line token caught up on the engine's steps. Now instead of running around the two vans of our train, Driver Ash put old *Ningwood* into reverse gear and we propelled our train up Apse Bank. After dropping off the token at

Wroxall, Frank went 'Hell for leather' to make up time and on arrival at St John's Road we were a mere five minutes late!

Jack Tharme

One summer Fred Brown, who was Signalman at Smallbrook Junction signal box, broke his fingers whilst accepting the single line staff from Driver Jack Sturgess as he passed by on his engine, No. 22 *Brading*. With no qualified signalman available to relieve poor Fred I was instructed to do Fred's duties, pulling the levers and undertaking the single line token/staff exchanges outside the box. The passing drivers were astonished to see me and decided to have a bit of fun by warming up the single line brass staffs on their shovels before handing them over to me, or making sure it thumped down on my hands like a schoolmaster's cane!

On another occasion early one morning, we were stopped at Ryde St John's Road and prevented from proceeding towards Smallbrook, as a flood had washed away the ballast from underneath the line at Smallbrook Junction. If we had gone over that section of track with the mail train we would have without doubt come off the line.

Wally Thrower

We were very keen on safety on the Island railways in those days and Ryde Pier Head station was provided with a pump for fire-fighting. I was an enthusiastic member of the fire-fighting team from about 1958 until 1962. In those days we would compete against other teams from railway centres like Eastleigh Works or Ashford Works in the regional fire-fighting competition, which was often as not held at Reigate in Surrey. We would practise each Wednesday evening at Ryde Pier Head using a Coventry Climax pump. The railway part-time team would receive assistance from Ryde Fire Brigade who also held their practice night on Wednesday evenings. If we won the regional competition (which we did), we then went on to the inter-regional competition. Sadly the team disbanded when staff cutbacks came in with closures. Prior to the competitions we would sharpen up and have a race against the professionals from Ryde and this lead to us winning the competition in 1960 and 1961, for the five-man trailer pump drill. May I add that we also entered a three-man hydrant drill team in all competitions. The waiting passengers at Ryde Pier Head would watch us and cheer, it also let them know that we were keen on safety.

Jack Tharme

Ryde Pier Head station could be a very dangerous place however as I well remember from my own bitter experience. One summer Saturday I climbed down off the platform to uncouple a six-coach Ventnor train in order that the O2 tank engine could run round the carriage set and head back towards St John's Road shed for servicing. As I uncoupled, I gave the 'all clear' to

The victorious Ryde Pier Head Station Fire Fighting Team, winners of the Inter-Regional Fire Fighting Challenge Shield for 1961, proudly displayed on return to the Island. Pictured left to right, back row Wally Thrower, Lofty Eklund, Harold Blundy, Jack Forrester. Front row Danny Heath and Jim Yeo.
Courtesy British Railways Board (Southern Region) Network SouthEast

the loco crew. I then caught hold of the carriage buffer to push myself up onto the platform. However, the carriage buffer had been pushed in and had remained compressed as a pin had broken. When I attempted to climb up and placed my weight on the compressed buffer it suddenly sprung out. This action resulted in me being catapulted through the air and eventually landing on the rail of the next platform line. I was immediately knocked out and was unconscious. Unfortunately the O2 tank was now heading straight towards my body and Driver Les King opened her regulator and whistled up to the signalman in the Pier Head box. At this point I could have been considered certain as a candidate for the undertaker. Driver King somehow caught sight of my body as his engine headed over the points and he shut the regulator and pulled the Westinghouse brake hard on. With an inch or so to spare he brought the locomotive to a stop and I was saved. They took me straight up to hospital where I recovered, but I owe my life to that driver.

Wally Thrower

From the operating point of view I agree Ryde Pier Head was a dangerous place to work. The platforms could only accommodate a six-carriage train set and a locomotive. Normally in the winter months the service trains to Ventnor and Cowes would consist of three-coach sets. Now the spare carriages and PMV vans were usually berthed in platform 1 along with two coke wagons which were brought to Ryde Pier Head with fuel for the central heating boilers. On this occasion my assignment was to shunt the locomotive and three coaches into platform 1 and collect two spare carriages for the school train. These two spare carriages were known to the railway staff as 'swingers'. I walked up the platform as the train propelled back the three-coach set, when suddenly, Roy Phythian held up his hand to halt us. I immediately signalled the same to the driver, but he just kept coming. After stopping, I climbed down and coupled up the two 'swingers'. We then pulled forward and set back into another platform, ready to depart. As I set about the usual pre-journey procedures, Roy Phythian walked up and said, "You've done it now. Look at those coke wagons on the buffer blocks at the end of platform 1". Sure enough the wagons had been pushed by our five coaches and locomotive right up and over the top of the buffer blocks! Well they had to bring out the Ryde Works breakdown train to recover those vehicles but strangely enough I never heard anything officially about the incident and I did not even have to write a report of what had happened. Nobody asked any questions and nothing was ever said.

In those days working with steam engines was hot and dirty work. Train crews required frequent refreshments, either a cup of tea or better still a pint of beer. Whenever I worked with Driver Jack Bradford he would regularly climb down off the footplate of his regular engine, No. 36 *Carisbrooke* at Ryde Pier Head and down a pint of beer in one to quench his thirst!

Jack Tharme

It was better still working with Driver Harry Peters on the footplate. If ever we had to wait at Wroxall for a 'fish and mail train' to pass, Harry would climb down off the footplate of his engine, No. 20 *Shanklin* and order drinks all round for fireman, guard and himself.

On the Island railways we had our own way of doing things in the running of the railway service. I remember resenting the interference of mainland railway staff who were posted to the Island following promotion. When Henry Powers the Area Inspector came over he had all sorts of weird and wonderful ways of running our railways, but one way he was put right by our boss Mr Gardiner. We entered Newport with a passenger train from Ryde, Denny Snow was the fireman on the locomotive and he had experienced problems with getting sufficient steam in the engine's boiler. This resulted in us coming to a dead halt and our only method of solving the problem was to work 'wrong line' into Newport station with assistance from an engine at the rear and remove our failed engine onto the shed. As guard, I gave permission for this to be carried out, and it meant that we continued with little loss of time. The next morning Mr Powers had me 'on the carpet' and gave me a lecture in wrong-line working. Mr Gardiner was sent for and he told the Area Inspector that the manoeuvre had been carried out within station limits and advised me to take no notice of this 'double track, main line Inspector!' If Island railway staff were left to get on with the job, there were no better railwaymen to be found on the system.

The Inter-Regional Fire Fighting Challenge Shield looks resplendent as it is proudly displayed in the forecourt of Ryde Pier Head station on 27th July 1961.
Courtesy British Railways Board (Southern Region)
Network SouthEast

Chapter Three – Permanent Way Stories

Tom Blackwell

If anyone had said that the Isle of Wight railways would be reduced to a mere stub from Ryde to Shanklin and a short preserved line from Haven Street when I started work on the Island railways in 1935, we would have laughed at them.

In those days there were over sixty miles of operating lines and I was part of the Newport permanent way gang. My very first assignment was to replace the points on the Haven Street station bridge one Saturday even-

ing. This was followed by a relaying job at Hunnyhill Viaduct just outside Newport on the Freshwater line. In the thirties there were extensive track improvements and I was happy to be a small part of it. The relaying of track on the Freshwater line continued slowly, but not without occasional drama. Returning from Carisbrooke one night with a heavily loaded redundant rail train of bolster wagons, the driver of the "Terrier" tank began to whistle furiously. His aim was to get the guard to apply his guard's van's brakes fully on. However the

A special permanent way relaying gang made up of railwaymen from all parts of the Island, seen here complete with hammers, new sleepers and pinch bars, just south of Smallbrook Junction on a Sunday morning in 1959. The ordinary gang of six to eight men has been strengthened to enable the work on the busy Smallbrook–Brading section to be completed in the shortest time possible. Pictured from left to right are Jim Hamilton, Sydney Dove, Fred Palmer, 'Taffy' Davis, Malcolm Jefferies, Bert Gould, unknown, Frank Budden, Rod Rood, unknown, Tom Scammell, Jack Kennedy, Jack Wheeler, and Johnny Rayner. On this occasion Jack Kennedy was the ganger in charge.
David Benning

Above: **The Ventnor West P. W. Gang pay their last respects to their branch locomotive and branch crew. Pictured left to right on engine No. 35 *Freshwater* are Malcolm Jefferies, Bill Lampard, Phil Record and Fireman Ken Simmonds. Standing left to right are George Sibbeck, Driver Jack Sewell and Joe Rew. On the other side of the camera was Guard Bill Symes.**
Malcolm Jefferies/Bill Lampard Collection

Above: **Tom Blackwell directs operations on Coppins Bridge and the removal of the drawbridge for the closed Sandown line at Newport.**

Tom Blackwell

Left: **Sunday morning finds Wroxall station a hive of activity with the 'down' line ballast being cleaned out ready for relaying.**
Bill Lampard/Bill Lewis Collection

113

speed of the train began to increase with sparks from the brake blocks showering out from the locomotive's wheels. The momentum of the heavy train pushed the reluctant "Terrier" past Newport North signal box and down Newport yards and eventually up and over the stop blocks. There was dust everywhere and hot steam gushed out of the locomotive from every point. We wandered down to inspect the "Terrier" which was perched at an angle of 45° and everyone just laughed and laughed.

Inspector Bill Macklen asked me to relay some points at Newport Yard and to supervise the relaying gang. This task was successful and I was given the job of organising relaying gangs on the Island railways, based at Newport. We would be expected to relay $\frac{1}{4}$ mile of line per night, approximately sixty lengths of track. The sections of line, chairs and fish plates were always dropped along the track proposed for relaying, ready for work to commence on the Saturday evening at 10.30pm. All relaying operations had to be concluded by 6.30am on the Sunday morning. Only once were we caught out when working at Yarmouth. Until the assignment had been completed, the train for Freshwater had to wait at Yarmouth. As a remarkable footnote to relaying on the Freshwater line, all brand new rail was put in along the entire length of the branch line in 1953. This must have been one of the very few occasions when the Island railways received new rail, yet very few trains travelled along its fourteen mile length. In 1953 the line closed and the Irish Government purchased the redundant rails.

One disadvantage of working in the Island relaying gangs was the need to withstand the results of lack of toilet facilities in Island carriage stock. When preparing to relay line at Carisbrooke Cutting on the Newport-Freshwater line, we would always be wary of the daily Ventnor-Freshwater limited stopping "Tourist" train, as passengers would regularly use this cutting to relieve themselves.

In steam days there were also many other disadvantages in that we had to use many different types of rail on the Island railways: Isle of Wight Railway, Isle of Wight Central Railway, London & South Western, and London, Brighton & South Coast Railways. We also had modern flat bottomed rail and even a short section of continental rail. The latter was an experimental type of rail and was laid between Shide and Blackwater. There were approximately thirty lengths of rail which were layed on concrete panels. The Southern Region regularly monitored this experiment but we were not informed of their findings.

The Island railways were always a source of improvisation. This was brought to bear following a flash flood after a thunderstorm. A torrent of water had washed along the trackbed near Cement Mills. It took with it wooden farm buildings and drowned livestock. The force of the water broke two stanchions supporting the Cement Mills Viaduct near Cowes. Temporary timber props were placed in to support the viaduct and the railway service was resumed. These temporary props remained in place until the line closed and are still in place today, some 25 years later!

Among the many amusing incidents I witnessed on the Island railways during relaying operations, there is one which sticks out. We were at Wroxall station replacing a pair of points opposite the bacon factory when the crane we were using began to sink down into the mud and became stuck. We managed to attach a heavy-duty chain to a locomotive and with much slipping and sparks the crane was hauled clear. If we hadn't been able to have pulled the crane out of the mud, she would have had to have been cut up there and then at Wroxall. As it turned out, tourists to the Island today can see this fine old crane preserved in all her glory at the Isle of Wight Steam Railway at Haven Street.

Bill Lampard

I worked in the humble permanent way department on the Island railways from 1951 until 1966. I started off in the Ventnor West gang and then transferred across to the main Ventnor-Sandown gang when the Ventnor West branch closed. The Ventnor West branch was not only the prettiest stretch of line on the Island but it was the best maintained stretch of track. Our ganger, George Silbeck insisted that every job was done to perfection and this resulted in us being awarded the, 'Trophy for the Best Kept Section of Permanent Way'. Now George was a real character and he would often be delayed at Dean Crossing where he would visit a lady friend for refreshments. Meanwhile the Ventnor West gang would be out checking the line up to Merstone and collecting

The Ventnor West P. W. Gang working on the track just outside Whitwell station towards Dean Crossing. Left to right are Joe Rew, Charlie Punt, Bill Lampard and George Sibbeck who is proudly showing the tear in his trouser leg where Charlie Punt has just stuck a pick axe through it!

Bill Lampard/Bill Lewis Collection

Above: **The award for the Eastleigh District 'Best Kept Length 1956 for The Greatest Improvement on D and E Class Lines' is awarded to the Brading Permanent Way Gang. This was largely due to the hard work of the former ganger for Brading 'Budder' Wheeler. Pictured left to right P. W. Inspector Macklen, Sub-Ganger Perce Lockyer, Alf Thomas, Ganger Jock Kennedy, Chief Engineer Restell, Tom H. Beckey, Charlie Punt, A. E. 'Burt' Gould and Jack W. Wheeler. The line had been previously inspected from the guard's compartment of a service train and walked by P. W. Inspector Macklen and found to be in outstanding condition.**

Courtesy British Rail

their catch of rabbits from pre-set snares along the side of the lines.

The main feature on the Ventnor-Sandown gang's stretch of line was the tunnel. We were provided with oil lamps for our passage through the tunnel. These were stored in pw huts at either end of the tunnel. We would walk through the tunnel every day checking for loose keys on the line. At weekends we would combine with the other Island pw gangs to meet at a set location for relaying, and over the years I have worked on every section of line in the Island.

Many of the embankments on the Island railways were built up with coal dust and ash. These always were a problem to pw gangs, and on one occasion, someone threw a match out of our hut at Shanklin after lighting a cigarette. The next thing we knew was that the coal dust caught and blazed away for some hours. We did

Left: **Tom Scammell (left) with Tom Beckey. These two Island railwaymen had just returned from Raynes Park Railway Gardening Competition where Tom Beckey had won the Southern Region Gardening Cup, which he proudly displays at Brading station.**

Tom Beckey Collection

115

try to put out the fire, but with some seven feet depth of coal dust there was little we could do.

During the winter we quite often had earth slips on the Wroxall side of Ventnor Tunnel. The embankment would fall in and distort the track or at the very least cover it in mud. This would half the passage of trains immediately until we had dug out and made repairs to the length. Likewise, water off the downs would cascade onto the track and the drainage system, unable to cope would cause severe flooding. This would wash away literally tons of ballast, leading to subsidence of the track.

It was interesting working on the line as we came into close contact with nature. Quite frequently we would catch adders and grass snakes, a popular place for them being between Hyde Road bridge outside Shanklin and Wroxall station.

There were only two real derailments in my time, one involving a shunting derailment at Shanklin which is mentioned in *Once Upon A Line Volume One*. The other derailment involved engine No. 22 *Brading* at Ventnor. After running forward to run round the carriage stock, Driver 'Mad' Jack Sturgess set the engine in reverse to run back over the points. The locomotive derailed on the points and her driving wheels slipped down onto the wooden sleepers. This created all sorts of problems and the breakdown gang had to be sent for from Ryde. Meanwhile two spare engines came down light to run the service.

When they closed the Ventnor-Shanklin section in 1966 I saw the red light and decided to leave the railway service.

Tom Beckey

When I started work in the permanent way gang at Merstone in September 1953 there was still quite a lot of the Island railway network remaining. The work was demanding, but the spirit of the men was second to none. My first winter on the railway was almost my last. It was a rather hard winter with a snow covering throughout the island. I remember one morning a forty-wagon loaded coal train from Medina Wharf hauled by a large Brighton E1 tank pulling into the platform at Merstone, where it halted to await the passage of a passing Sandown-Newport passenger train. As it was so cold and frosty I decided to seek out the two largest lumps of coal from a wagon off the coal train and take them up to Signalman Syd Dennett up in Merstone signal box for his fire. About an hour later the station master at Sandown telephoned to find out who had helped themselves to some coal from his loaded wagons. But how had he discovered my misdemeanour I wondered. He informed me that there were two large black holes in the white, snow covered wagons!

We were always glad to see the back of the winter on the Sandown-Newport line, but spring also brought its trials and tribulations to the line. Each spring there would be flooding during the end of March and April owing to the stream running alongside Alverstone station over-flowing its banks. The water level would rise after heavy rainfalls and spill out over the adjacent railway line. The depth of water could be as much as three feet. Local residents would canoe over the railway line! Of course the train service had to be suspended when flooding occurred. Our ganger at Merstone, Perce Buckett, could predict almost to the minute when flooding would occur and when the line should be closed, by working out high tide times.

Sadly, the Sandown-Newport line closed in 1956 and I transferred to the Brading permanent way gang. The line here, from Ryde to Ventnor was particularly busy and it was full of colourful railway characters. It wasn't long before I became acquainted with one Driver 'Mad' Jack Sturgess and his locomotive No. 22 *Brading*. He

Tom Scammell — Percy Trimmer & Jack Tharme. are all expert Horticulturists, & are very often in competition with each other.

Guard – "Vic Lacey"

would regularly pass by on No. 22 and empty the remains of his tea pot over the Brading gang. His engine was driven as if there was no tomorrow. On one such occasion 22 roared past us and we retreated back into the lineside undergrowth, but 'Mad' Jack had the last laugh, for about five minutes after 22 had gone past, we heard a fire engine. We decided to wander down the line to investigate what all the commotion was about. To our dismay we discovered that some sparks from the exhaust from old *Brading's* Drummond chimney had set our pw hut alight which by now was completely gutted and it had contained my clean shirt!

I had experienced flooding on the Sandown-Newport line as mentioned earlier, but this was nothing to that which greeted me one morning at Smallbrook Junction. During the night there had been heavy rain, resulting in flooding at Ryde St John's Road shed, works, station and tunnel. At Smallbrook the water from a culvert spilled out and washed away the ballast. It was possible to stand up under the track which was suspended in mid-air. One of the first on the scene was Tom Blackwell who quickly organised the Ryde and Brading gangs into an effective combined team to repair the damage. Heavy sand bags were piled up in columns to support the precarious sleepers and rails. Next, Tom wedged rocks and sleepers underneath to add extra strength to his packing until more substantial repairs could be made. Within six hours trains were running over this Heath Robinson emergency repair – albeit at 5 mph. Within a week Sid Newbury and Tom Blackwell had filled in the empty crater with shingle, locomotive ash and ballast.

Working on the permanent way helped me to appreciate nature in all its forms as this anecdote will reveal.

One morning Signalman Harold Fry told me to take a shovel with me when walking the Ventnor-Shanklin section of line, as a loco crew had reported hitting a dog. As I approached Cliff Road bridge I discovered a dead badger which had been struck by a passing train. I dug out a two foot hole and duly buried it. The next morning I was on the same line patrol and discovered that the badger's grave had been excavated and the creature's remains were gone! I continued my long routine patrol and strolled up Apse Bank wondering what could have happened to the poor dead badger. At Three Arch bridge cutting, which was some way on from Cliff Road bridge, I spotted the dead badger's body on the right-hand side of the line. On the left-hand side of the line was another dead badger which I presume must have been his mate. The female badger had dragged the dead body of her companion along the track and had attempted to return his remains to the set but in so doing had been hit by another train herself.

An annual event in steam days on the Isle of Wight was the annual pigeon specials to Ventnor. A train of vans would arrive at Ventnor packed with pigeon baskets. In between services the station staff and pw staff would release the captive birds at a given signal. This flight would hopefully teach the pigeons to become accustomed to crossing water on their return home.

The Isle of Wight is always thought of by many as the 'Sunshine Isle', but I recall the night when it was anything but. I was just about to book off duty to return home. Signalman Eddie Spears was about to close

"watch the birdie"

Guard Ron Childs could be seen with a shunting pole in one hand, & a camera in the other. He was very good with both.

Shanklin signal box for the night and set the points and signals ready for the next morning's mail train. Suddenly the sky began to turn white and all fell silent. He experienced great difficulty in opening the points at the Sandown end of Shanklin station and asked me to assist. I cleaned the points and tried to crow bar them across, but the snow was falling too fast. In the end we had to give up and set three warning detonators on the line for approaching trains. The next morning the Isle of Wight looked like a Christmas card with an arctic landscape. The next train to pass through Shanklin, the morning mail train hauled by No. 29 *Alverstone* did not reach Shanklin until 6pm at night.

In closing my memories, spare a final thought next time you see a vintage steam train for the permanent way railwayman of yesteryear, for he was truly the unsung hero of the Island railways. One such hero of those bygone days was Ganger Albert 'Budder' Wheeler. He was a dedicated railwayman whom I recall one day crawling into a leaking pipe which required some repairs as its contents were discharging onto the railway line. When he had completed this unpleasant assignment I remember him crawling out into the fresh air, looking a somewhat darker colour than which he had commenced the job. Upon returning home to Brading station we were greeted by Mrs Wheeler. "Phew! Is that our Albert?" she enquired. "Yes". I replied. To which Mrs Wheeler retorted, "Well he had better not come home smelling and looking like that. He can jump in the river!"

Guard Sam Wells, now a very keen Motorist.

Below and right: **Three unique views of the flood damage at Smallbrook Junction as described by Tom Beckey.**

Tom Beckey

ENGINE DUTIES : NEWPORT DEPOT : SATURDAYS ONLY, COMMENCING 6th JUNE, 1953.

arr.No.20(O2.Class)dep.

	N.	8.43am
9.19am	R.	9.35
10. 8	N.	10||15
10||20	Loco.	12||10pm
12||15pm	N.	12.40
1.12	F.	1.20
1.59	N.	2.39
3.13	R.	3.42
4.32	V.	4.40
5.23	R.	6.10
6.52	V.	7||15
7||30	Sln.	8.35Ft.
10.15	N.	–

1st set on 7.40am, Rlf.
2.35pm, also Requirements
No. 19.
2nd set on 2.20pm, disposal
by 4.0pm "AO".

arr.No.21(O2.Class)dep.

	Loco.	2|| 5pm
	N.	2||10
2||40pm	R.	3.10
3.52	V.	4.20
5. 1	R.	5.35
6. 6	N.	6||10
6||15	Loco.	7|| 0
7||5	N.	7.10
7.46	F.	7.55
8.32	N.	9.10
9.46	F.	9||55
10||25	N.	–

Men on 12.50pm,
Rlf. 8.35pm by 7.30pm
"AO".

arr.No.22(E1.Class)dep.

	N. FS.	4.40am
	N.	5.~0Ft
5.10am	M.W.	5.40
5.45	G.H.S.	6. 5
6.10	M.W.	
FS. 6.10 – 9.15am.		
	M.W.	9.15
9.22	C.	
FS. 9.22 – 10. 9		
	C.	10. 9
10.15 or)	M.W.	
10.27Q.)		FS.7.~0pm
7.12pm	N. FS.| 7||45
7||50	Loco.	–

Engine to take require-
ments at Medina Wharf
at convenient time.

1st set on 3.50am, Rlf.
@ M.W. 12.18pm.
Pass. to N. 12.30pm.
2nd set on 11.53am,
Pass. to M.W. 12. 8pm.

arr.No.23(O2.Class)dep.

	Loco.	2||55pm
3|| 0pm	N.	3. 8
3.19	C.	3.53
4.40	S.	5. 3
5.49	C.	5.56
6.38	S.	7. 3
7.49	C.	7.56
8.38	S.	9. 8
9.35	N.	–

Men on 2.10pm.

NOTES :

X – Loco. Requirements.
CS – Coaching Shunting.
FS – Freight Shunting.
DS – Departmental Shunting.
AO – As Ordered.
  S.W. SMART,
SUPT. OF OPERATION.
  per:

NEWPORT, I.W. A.D.T.S.O.
20.5.53.

Sheet No.2.

BRITISH RAILWAYS
SOUTHERN REGION

ENGINE DUTIES : NEWPORT DEPOT : SUNDAYS, COMMENCING 7th JUNE, 1953.

arr.No.13(02.Class)dep.		
	N.	6.20am
6.55am	N.	7.15
8. 4	C.	8.25
8.56	N.	9.38
9.49	C.	9.56
10.41	S.	11.38
11.55	N.	11.45
11.50	Loco.	12.55pm
1. 0pm	N.	1. 8
1.19	C.	1.26
1.37	N.	1.45
1.50	Loco.	2.50
2.55	N.	3. 8
3.49	C.	3.56
4.21	S.	5. 8
5.49	C.	5.56
6.56	S.	6.50
7.16	N.	–

1st set on 5.20am.
  Rlf. 1. 5pm.
2nd set on 12.50pm.

arr.No.14(02.Class)dep.		
	N.	CS.8.25am
	N.	8.43
9.18am	R.	9.35
10.19	C.	10.26
11.13	R.	11.35
12.19pm	C.	12.26pm
1.13	R.	1.35
2. 6	N.	
CS. 2.6 – 2.20pm.		
	N.	2.20
2.25	Loco.	3.55
4.0	N.	4.10
4.47	F.	4.55
5.32	N.	6. 8
6.19	C.	6.26
7.13	R.	7.35
8. 6	N.	8.50
9.27	F.	9.34
10.10	N.	–

1st set on 7.35am.
  Rlf. 3.10pm.
2nd set on 2.55pm.

NEWPORT, I.W.,
A.D.T.S.O.
20.5.53.

arr.No.15(02.Class)dep.		
	N.	8. 8am)
8.19am	C.	8.25)Q.
8.56	N.	)
	N.	9. 8
9.19	C.	9.26
9.37	N.	CS.
	N.	10.40
11.16	F.	11.25
12. 2pm	N.	12. 9pm
12.38	S.	1.50
2.35	C.	2.43
2.54	N.	3. 0
3. 5	Loco.	5.15
5.20	N.	5.40
6.16	F.	6.25
7. 3	N.	7.18
7.44	S.	7.50
8.29	C.	8.36
9.20	R.	9.35
10. 6	N.	–

1st set on 6.30am.
  Shed shunting and
  above until 3. 7pm.
2nd set on 2.50pm.

arr.No.16(02.Class)dep.		
	N.	8.10am
8.40am	F.	8.50
9.32	N.	9.39
10.15	R.	10.35
11.19	C.	11.26
12.13pm	R.	12.35pm
1. 6	N.	1.10
1.15	Loco.	2.25
2.30	N.	2.42
3.13	R.	3.35
4. 6	N.	4.10
4.15	Loco.	5.20
5.25	N.	5.39
6.13	R.	6.35
7.19	C.	7.26
8.13	R.	8.42
9.29	C.	9.36
9.47	N.	–

1st set on 7.10am.
  Rlf. 2.40pm.
2nd set on 2.25pm.

arr.No.17(02.Class)dep.		
	N.	CS.11. 5am
	N.	12.40pm
1.16pm	F.	1.35
2.13	N.	2.20
2.55	F.	3.25
4. 2	N.	4.15
4.20	Loco.	7. 5
7.10	N.	7.20
7.57	F.	8. 5
8.42	N.	8.50
9.24	Skn.	9.32
9.36	S.	9.50
10.29	C.	10.36
10.47	N.	–

1st set on 10.15am.
  Rlf. 5.50pm.
2nd set on 5.30pm and
  Shed Marshalling.

NOTES :

X – Loco.
    Requirements.
CS – Coaching
    Shunting.

S.W. SMART.
SUPT. OF OPERATION.
  per:-

120

ENGINE DUTIES : NEWPORT DEPOT : WEEKDAYS (S.X.) COMMENCING 8th JUNE, 1953.

arr.No.13(O2.Class)dep.

arr.		dep.
	N.	4.40am
4.52am	S.	6.37
7.21	R.	7.30
7.35	RSJ.	
	CS/FS.	
	RSJ.	9.0
9.5	R.	9.55
10.8	N.	10.45
11.16	F.	11.24
12.1pm	N.	12.10pm
12.15	Loco.	2.15
2.20	N.	2.39
3.13	R.	3.35
4.19	C.	4.26
5.13	R.	5.35
6.6	N.	6.10
6.15	Loco.	7.0
7.5	N.	7.10
7.46	F.	7.55
8.32	N.	8.40
9.16	F.	9.30Ft
10.13	N.	-

1st set on 3.40am, Rlf. 12.1pm by 1st set of 21.
2nd set on 1.15pm, Rlf. 8.40pm by 7.30pm "AO".
M. and Th - Disposal by 3rd set of 14.

arr.No.14(O2.Class)dep.

arr.		dep.
	N.	4.50amFt.
5.37am	F.	7.50
8.35	N.	9.1
9.39	F.	10.0
10.34	N.	11.17
11.53	F.	12.0nn
12.35pm	N.	12.40pm
12.45	Loco.	2.5
2.10	CS. N.	2.40
3.16	F.	3.25
4.2	N.	
	CS. &/or FS.Q.	
	N.	5.10
5.49	F.	6.22
7.2	N.	7.9
7.38	S.	8.8
8.49	C.	8.56
9.7	N.	-

1st set on 3.50am, Rlf. 11.10am.
2nd set on 11.0am, Rlf. 5.0pm, and clean Shed engine fire.
3rd set on 4.0pm, also dispose of No.13 M. and Th.

arr.No.15(O2.Class)dep.

arr.		dep.
	N.	5.50am
	CS., FS. &/or DS.	
	N.	7.50 Q.Ft
8.18am	S.	8.40 Q.Ft
9.5	M.	9.13 Van.
	N.	8.40 Q.Ft
8.25	M.	9.13 Van.
OR	N.	8.20
8.30	M.	9.13 Van.
9.25	N.	
	R-R Van.	
	N.	9.41
10.13	R.	10.35
11.19	C.	11.26
11.37	N. CS.	
	N.	12.40pm
1.16pm	F.	2.0
2.34	N.	2.35
2.40	Loco.	3.40
3.45	N.	4.9
4.45	F.	5.20
5.54	N.	6.15
6.51	F.	7.17
7.57	N.	-

1st set on 5.0am, Rlf. 12.40pm.
2nd set on 12.25pm.

arr.No.16(O2.Class)dep.

arr.		dep.
	N.	6.20am
6.34am	C.	6.56
7.49	S.	8.23
8.51	N.	9.38
9.49	C.	10.3
10.47	S.	11.8
11.49	C.	11.56
12.38pm	S.	1.8pm
1.35	N.CS.	1.45
1.50	Loco.	2.50
2.55	N.	3.15
3.55	F.	4.15
4.54	N.	4.55
5.0	Loco.	5.55
6.0	N.	6.8
6.19	C.	6.26
7.13	R.	7.35
8.19	C.	8.26
9.13	R.	9.35
10.19	C.	10.26
10.37	N.	-

1st set on 5.20am, Rlf. 1.50pm.
2nd set on 1.35pm, Rlf. 10.6pm by 2nd set of 20.

arr.No.17(O2.Class)dep.

arr.		dep.
	N.	7.39am
8.11am	R.	8.25
9.11	C.	9.26
9.37	N.	
	CS., FS &/or DS.	
	N.	11.39
12.13pm	R.	12.35pm
1.6	N.	1.10
1.15	Loco.	2.20
2.25	CS. N.	2.38
2.49	C.	3.26
4.13	R.	4.35
5.19	C.	5.26
6.13	R.	6.35
7.6	N.	7.38
7.49	C.	7.56
8.38	S.	9.8
9.35	N.	-

1st set on 6.35am, Rlf. 2.25pm.
2nd set on 2.10pm.

arr.No.18(O2.Class)dep.

arr.		dep.
	N.	8.12am
8.24am	C.	8.43
9.34	Skn.	9.43
10.30	C.	10.56
11.38	S.	12.8pm
12.49pm	C.	12.56
1.38	S.	2.8
2.35	N.	2.40
2.45	Loco.	3.25
3.30	N.	3.38
4.49	C.	4.56
5.38	S.	5.51
6.5	Mor.	6.23
6.49	C.	7.26
8.13	R.	8.35
9.19	C.	9.26
9.37	N.	-

1st set on 7.10am, Rlf. 2.55pm.
2nd set on 2.40pm.

Continued to

arr.No.19(O2.Class)dep.
```
             N.       1. 8pm
1.19pm     C.         1.26
2.13       R.         2.35
3.19       C.         3.53
4.40       S.         5. 8
5.49       C.         5.56
6.38       S.         7. 8
7.35       N.          -
```
Men on 12. 5pm,
    disposal by 2nd set
    of No. 21.

arr.No.20(El.Class)dep.
```
    On Main Line 4.40am.FS.
             N.       5. 0 Ft.
5.10am    M.W.        5.40
5.45      G.H.S.      6. 5
6.10      M.W.
    FS. 6.10 - 9.15am.
             M.W.     9.15 Ft.
9.22       C.
FS. 9.22-9.52 or 10.32.Q.
           C.(        9.52 Ft.
9.58 or)       (or 10.32.Q.
10.50.Q.)M.W.
    FS. to 1.39pm.
             M.W.     1.39 Ft.
1.50pm     N.    FS.2.25
2.30       Loco.     5. 0
5. 5       N.    FS.5.48 Ft.
6.38       RSJ. FS.8.15 Ft.
8.53       N.
    FS to 9.15pm.
```
1st set on 3.50am, Rlf. M.W.
11.18am by 7.0am "AO". Pass
to M.W. 11. 9am.
2nd set on 4. 0pm, also No.16
from 10. 6pm.
NEWPORT, I.W. A.D.T.S.O.,
20.5.53.

Sheet No.2.

arr.No.21(El.Class)dep.
```
             N.       6.25am.Ft.
8.53am     V.
    FS. 8.53 - 9.50am.
           V.         10. 0
10.41      N.         10 50
10 55      Loco.      11 0pm
11 5pm     N.
    CS &/or FS.
             N.       1.53 Ft.
2. 5       M.W. FS.7. 0 Ft.
7.12       N.
    FS. until 7.30pm.Q.
```
1st set on 5.25am, also
    No. 13 from 12. 1pm.
2nd set on 12.45pm, also
    dispose of No. 19.

arr.No.22(El.Class)dep.
```
           N. CS.     5.20pm
           N.         5.57
6.42pm     V.         7.15 Ft.
9.15       N.
    FS. until 10. 0pm.Q.
```
Men on 4.30pm, also
    Shed Marshalling.

NOTES :

X - Loco. Requirements.
CS - Coaching Shunting.
FS - Freight Shunting.
DS - Departmental Shunting.
AO - As Ordered.

S.W. SMART,
SUPT. OF OPERATION,
    per:-

CI

INDEX

NOTES

(i) Where no separate time is shown for arrival and departure, the time indicated is the departure time, small type indicates passing time.

(ii) Trains must leave at the advertised times whenever practicable. Where the advertised departure times of passenger trains are slightly earlier than those shown in the Working Time Table, the former must be used in all quotations to the public.

(iii) 15 seconds are allowed for station duties in the case of passenger trains unless separate arrival and departure times are provided, or more time is specified by letter indications.

EXPLANATION OF REFERENCES

M	...	Monday	Th	...	Thursday
T	...	Tuesday	F	...	Friday
W	...	Wednesday	S	...	Saturday

The addition of the letter "**O**" indicates that the train will run on that day or those days only.
The letter "**X**" indicates that the train will not run on that day or those days.

AE — Stops only to attach or detach assisting engine.
D — Stops only to set down (passenger trains), or detach (freight trains).
E — Stops only for examination.
ECS — Empty coaching stock train.
†F — Stops only for working purposes, if running late stop not to be made.
L — Stops only to change engine or trainmen.
LE — Light engine.
P — Stops only to pin down or pick up wagon brakes.
Q — Runs when required.
R — Stops when required.
U — Stops only to take up (passenger trains), or to attach (freight trains).
W — Stops only for water.
X — Indicates points at which trains are booked to cross each other on a single line at a crossing place.
‡.• — Advertised time in public time table.
— Stops or shunts for other trains to pass.
↓↑ — For continuation of train timings, see subsequent column.
— Train timings continued from previous column.

a	— Arrives 1 minute earlier.	f	— Arrives 3½ minutes earlier.
b	— " 1½ " "	g	— " 4 " "
c	— " 2 minutes earlier.	h	— " 4½ " "
d	— " 2½ " "	j	— " 5 " "
e	— " 3 " "		

British Railways

SOUTHERN REGION

SOUTH WESTERN DIVISION

WORKING TIME TABLE

of

PASSENGER AND FREIGHT TRAINS

ISLE OF WIGHT

14th JUNE, 1965, to 4th SEPTEMBER, 1966, or until further notice

IMPORTANT NOTICE—MAXIMUM SPEED OF TRAINS

Trains must not exceed a MAXIMUM speed of 40 miles per hour at any point and all restrictions which impose a lower speed must be strictly observed.

MAKING UP TIME

When trains are running late, Drivers must endeavour to make up time with due regard to the braking power of the engine and train, provided that all speed restrictions are strictly complied with and that the maximum speed shown above is not exceeded.

F. P. B. TAYLOR,
Line Manager.

WIMBLEDON

SECTION C

READY RECKONER

No. of Wagons	Heavy	13 tons and under		
		Medium	Light	Empty
1	1½	1	1	½
2	3	1½	1	2
3	5	3	2	3
4	7	6	4	3
5	8	7	5	4
6	10	9	6	5
7	12	10	8	6
8	13	11	8	7
9	15	13	10	8
10	17	14	10	8
11	18	16	12	9
12	20	17	12	10
13	22	19	13	11
14	23	20	14	12
15	25	21	15	13

No. of Wagons	Heavy	13 tons and under		
		Medium	Light	Empty
16	27	23	16	13
17	28	24	17	14
18	30	26	18	15
19	32	27	19	16
20	33	29	20	17
21	35	30	21	18
22	37	31	22	18
23	38	33	23	19
24	40	34	24	20
25	42	36	25	21
26	43	37	26	22
27	45	39	27	23
28	47	40	28	23
29	48	41	29	24
30	50	43	30	25

METHOD OF CALCULATING FREIGHT TRAIN LOADS

The method of calculation described in Sections 1 to 3 below is applicable throughout British Railways.

1. INDICATION OF LOAD CATEGORY

All loaded wagons originating in Great Britain bear prominently on the wagon label a letter 'H', 'M' or 'L', indicating the load categories 'Heavy', 'Medium' or 'Light'.

It will be the duty of the labelling staff to determine the load category of each wagon according to the definitions given below and to affix the correct wagon label inserting where necessary the appropriate letter in the space provided.

In cases where there has been a failure to do this and it is not possible to determine the classification of wagon load from examination of other detail on the label, the wagon it to be treated as 'HEAVY' for the purpose of load calculation.

2. DEFINITIONS OF 'HEAVY', 'MEDIUM', AND 'LIGHT' CATEGORIES

	When nett load is	
	Wagons of 13 tons capacity or under	Wagons of over 13 tons capacity
Heavy	10 tons and over	⅔ and over carrying capacity
Medium	6 tons and under 10 tons	⅓ and under ⅔ carrying capacity
Light	Under 6 tons	Under ⅓ carrying capacity

3. CALCULATION OF TRAIN LOADS

A wagon of 13 tons (or under) capacity containing a load weighing under 6 tons (i.e. bearing 'L' indication on label) will be regarded as the Basic Wagon Unit and all train loads are quoted in terms of Basic Wagon Units.

For wagons of up to 13 tons capacity, the equation connecting the different load categories is :—

10 'Light' (i.e. Basic Wagon Units)
equals 7 'Medium'
equals 6 'Heavy'
equals 12 'Empty'

For wagons of higher capacity, similar relationships apply, and the following shows the approximate equivalents in terms of BASIC WAGON UNITS :—

Marked Carrying Capacity	Equivalent Basic Wagon Units			
	Heavy	Medium	Light	Empty*
13 tons and under	1⅔	1¼	1	†

NOTES :

(a) **Train Brake Van**

Not to be counted as part of load. (For this purpose the train brake van is to be considered as being only that vehicle in which the Guard is riding.)

(b) **Runner or Match Wagons**

Runner or match wagons f— long and projecting loads should be classified as empty for load calculating purposes but must be shown as loaded wagons on guards journals.

(c) **Additional Brake Vans, Brake Tenders, Coaching Stock, etc.**

Travelling cranes, 'dead' engines, etc. to be also calculated on this basis.

To be calculated on tare weight, each 12 tons equal to one Basic Unit.

RESTRICTIONS AS TO THE RUNNING OF ENGINES OVER CERTAIN PORTIONS OF THE LINE.

The following engines must not be run over the undermentioned Section of the Line:—

Nos. of Engines	Section of Line
Nos. W14, W16-W18, W21-W22, W24, W26-W31, W33 and W35	Cement Mills Siding.

CLASSIFICATION OF ENGINES

(ISLE OF WIGHT SECTION)

Load Class	Engine Numbers
B	W14, W16-W18, W21-W22, W24, W26-W31, W33 and W35

PASSENGER TRAINS

SECTION OF LINE		Class of Engine B		REMARKS
From	To	Tons		
Newport	Cowes	187		D—When good weather conditions prevail the loads of these trains may be increased to 160 tons.
Cowes	Newport	155D		
Newport	Ryde	155D		
Ryde	Newport			
Ventnor	Ryde			

LOADS OF FREIGHT TRAINS IN THE ISLE OF WIGHT

The table shown below is given as a basis for the number of wagons to be worked on Freight trains, but there may be exceptional circumstances requiring one or two more wagons to be sent forward. To prevent extra running in such cases, it is expected that all concerned will co-operate towards obtaining the best results.

During the prevalence of strong winds, hard frosts, or a slippery state of rails, the authorised loads are subject to a reduction and two, three or more wagons to prevent the locomotive coming to a stand, and when such reduction is necessary, the Driver must advise the Guard in good time before starting, so that arrangements may be made accordingly.

FREIGHT TRAINS

SECTION OF LINE		Maximum Load inclusive of Van	Class of Engine B		REMARKS
From	To	Limit	Equivalent to Basic Wagon Units		
Newport	Medina Wharf ...		45	25	
Medina Wharf ...	Cowes		30	25	
Cowes	Medina Wharf ...		40	26	
Newport	Ryde		40	30	
Ryde	Newport		40	40	
Ryde	Ventnor		40	40	
Ventnor	Ryde		40	30	

GENERAL INSTRUCTIONS

INSTRUCTIONS FOR THE GUIDANCE OF GOODS GUARDS IN THE COMPILATION OF THE FREIGHT TRAIN JOURNAL

The Freight Train Journal is one of the principal documents upon which the British Railways statistics are based, and in order that full credit may be taken for the work done it is of great importance that these necessary details should be correctly given in clear handwriting.

The following instructions should be adhered to by Guards so that there shall be no difficulty in filling in the necessary details correctly :—

GENERAL

(a) Freight Train Journals should be used for freight trains for all trips of half a mile or over beyond the limits of a yard or station.

(b) Completed Journals to be sent to the Line Manager's Office, Newport, IW.

HEADING OF JOURNAL

(a) Class of train

The Class of train to be shown, and, if the class of train as run is different from the class booked to run the Guard should give the reason in the remarks section at the bottom of the journal.

(b) Freight train from......................to........

The Freight Train Journal to relate normally to one train only but where instructions exist that the journal should be used for more than one train the title of the second or further train should be clearly shown in the body of the journal except in the case of a series of short trips when it will suffice if the title of the first trip only is shown in the space provided at the top of the form.

(c) The day of the week and the date of the booked departure from starting point of the train to be recorded.

(d) W.T.T. or Train Number.

To be shown when such information appears in the Working Time Table. The letters 'SPL' should be shown when the train is a Special.

COLUMNS OF JOURNALS

Column 1

Particulars to be inserted showing the information called for at the head of the column and in addition all points where the train is stopped for any reason, including signal stops, to be recorded. Where the Working Time Table gives particulars of passing points these also to be shown in this column together with passing times.

Column 2

The booked and actual times and minutes late to be shown in respect of appropriate items in Column 1 also the line on which run, e.g. fast, slow, through, etc.

Column 3

The actual time only (in minutes) occupied, i.e. from commencing shunting operations until the engine is back again, coupled to its train ready to resume the journey, is to be shown.

If an engine puts its own train into a siding or on to another road without attaching or detaching any vehicles, in order to allow another train to pass, the time so occupied is NOT to be shown as shunting.

Column 4

The Signal name or number to be recorded, and all signal delays must be shown although the train may arrive at or pass its next timing point on or before time.

Column 6

Minutes occupied under the following headings should be included in this column, the actual cause being shown.

P.W. checks.
C. & W. examinations.
Changing train crews.
Waiting booked assisting or bank engine, etc.

Columns 8, 9 and 10 (general notes as to recording of vehicles)

Loaded wagons to be recorded as under :—

Column 8		Column 9		Column 10				
Wagons attached		Wagons detached		No. of wagons Leaving each point				
Loaded	Empty	Loaded	Empty	Loaded	Equal B.W.U.	Empty	Departmental Full train load	Total B.W.U.
...	...	...	...	...	...	...	...	...

Train Brake Vans NOT to be included unless running Engine and Brake Van only, when the remark 'E. & B.' should be inserted in the 'Empty' Column in section 10.

Spare Brake Vans to be shown as 'Empty' wagons in Columns 8, 9 and 10. Guards are asked to record in the 'Remarks' section the points between which these spare brake vans are conveyed.

Guard, runner, or match wagons when in use as such to be treated as loaded wagons.

Coaching vehicles loaded or empty to be included.

Ryde, Sandown, Ventnor, Newport and Cowes

MONDAYS TO FRIDAYS

C5

DOWN

Mileage			PORTSMOUTH Hbr. } Boat RYDE PIER }		1	2	Freight to Ventnor	Mail	Mail	LE	Stops Cement Mills when required	Freight	Freight	
M	C	C												
0	0	0	RYDE PIER HEAD ... dep		03 05			04 05	04 10					06 00
0	32	32	RYDE PIER ... dep		03 35									06 30
1	10	2	Esplanade				04 03							
2	10	0	St. John's Road				04 13		05 00					06 44
4	54		Smallbrook Jn.						05 43					06 49
			Brading ... arr					04 30						06 55
			dep					04 30						06 55
6	41		Sandown ... arr					04 35						07 04
			dep					04 38						07 05
8	28		Shanklin ... arr											07 06
			dep											07 07
11	3		Wroxall ... arr					04 51						07 15
			dep											07 15
12	44		VENTNOR ... arr				04 32		06 00		04 55			07 20
	3	71	Ashey								06 15	06 51	06 23	
	5	35	Havenstreet								R	06 59	06 37	
9		77	NEWPORT ... arr				04 44				06 29	07 01		07 05
	13	9	Medina Wharf ... dep											07 15
	13	42	Gas Works Siding											
	13	68	Mill Hill											
	14	24	COWES ... arr				04 55							

DOWN

PORTSMOUTH Hbr. } Boat RYDE PIER }		1	2	Freight to Ventnor	Mail	Mail	LE	Stops Cement Mills	ECS	G	MXQ	Pcls	
RYDE PIER HEAD ... dep		04 35	07 07	07 40		07 40				07 55			
RYDE PIER ... dep		07 05	07 07	07 45		07 45	07 55		08 04				
Esplanade			07 11	07 49		07 49		08 00	08 11				
St. John's Road			07 15							09 25			
Smallbrook Jn.										08 13			
Brading ... arr			07 16	07 50		07 50		08 09	08 19				
dep			07 18			07 55		08 09	08 21				
Sandown ... arr			07 22	07 58		07 58		08 15	08 25				
dep			07 30	08 00		08 00		08 18	08 27				
Shanklin ... arr			07 33	08 10		08 10		08 26	08 34				
dep			07 37			08 15		08 34	08 42				
Wroxall ... arr			07 44	08 24		08 24		08 47	08 53				
dep			07 49	08 29		08 29		08 53	08 55				
VENTNOR ... arr			07 54						09 00				
Ashey			07 22								09 02		
Havenstreet			07 24								09 08		
NEWPORT ... arr			07 37				09 38				09 21		
Medina Wharf ... dep			07 41										
Gas Works Siding			R										
Mill Hill			07 52										
COWES ... arr			07 54										

DOWN

PORTSMOUTH Hbr. } Boat RYDE PIER }		1	2	EBV	G	ECS	G	Withheld minutes				
RYDE PIER HEAD ... dep		08 35	08 50	09 30	09 25	09 45	09 30	10 25	10 30			10 38
RYDE PIER ... dep		09 05	08 55	09 34	09 29	09 45	09 50	10 29	10 34			11 08
Esplanade				09 38	09 33			10 33	10 38			
St. John's Road						10 00						
Smallbrook Jn.								10 37	10 41			
Brading ... arr				09 41	09 41			10 39	10 42			
dep				09 46	09 46			10 42	10 46			
Sandown ... arr				09 53	09 53		10 12	10 48	10 50			
dep				09 56	09 56			10 48	10 56			
Shanklin ... arr				10 04	10 04			10 47	11 04			
dep				10 08	10 08			10 52	11 12			
Wroxall ... arr				10 12	10 12			11 44	11 52			
VENTNOR ... arr				10 45		09 50						
Ashey				09 48	09 50	10 04	10 38	10 41			
Havenstreet				10 00	10 00	10 21	11 00				
NEWPORT ... arr				10 13				10 50	11 13			
Medina Wharf ... dep				10 15				10 52	11 15			
COWES ... arr												

MONDAYS TO FRIDAYS, 14th JUNE to 3rd SEPTEMBER, 1965 and 13th JUNE to 2nd SEPTEMBER, 1966

C7 — MONDAYS TO FRIDAYS

Ryde, Sandown, Ventnor, Newport and Cowes

SATURDAYS, 19th JUNE to 4th SEPTEMBER, 1965 and 4th JUNE to 3rd SEPTEMBER, 1966

SATURDAYS

Commences 17th July 1965 and 16th July 1966

C6 — MONDAYS TO FRIDAYS

MONDAYS TO FRIDAYS, 14th JUNE to 3rd SEPTEMBER, 1965 and 13th JUNE to 2nd SEPTEMBER, 1966

Ryde, Sandown, Ventnor, Newport and Cowes

DOWN

	PORTSMOUTH Hbr. } Boat
	RYDE PIER } dep
	RYDE PIER HEAD ... dep
	Esplanade
	St. John's Road
	Smallbrook Jn.
	Brading ... arr
	dep
	Sandown ... arr
	dep
	Shanklin ... arr
	dep
	Wroxall ... arr
	dep
	VENTNOR ... arr
	Ashey ... dep
	Havenstreet
	NEWPORT ... arr
	dep
	Medina Wharf
	Gas Works Siding
	Mill Hill
	COWES ... arr

SATURDAYS, 19th JUNE to 4th SEPTEMBER, 1965 and 4th JUNE to 3rd SEPTEMBER, 1966

SATURDAYS

DOWN

Commences 17th July, 1965 and 16th July, 1966

Ryde Esplanade arr. 06.57

Scops Cement Mills when required

C9 — SATURDAYS

Ryde, Sandown, Ventnor, Newport and Cowes

(DOWN timetable; three panels of departure/arrival columns)

Stations (rows):

1. PORTSMOUTH Hbr. }Boat — dep
2. RYDE PIER — dep
3. RYDE PIER HEAD — dep
4. Esplanade
5. St. John's Road
6. Smallbrook Jn.
7. Brading — arr
8. — dep
9. Sandown — arr
10. — dep
11. Shanklin — arr
12. — dep
13. Wroxall — arr
14. — dep
15. VENTNOR — arr
16. Ashey
17. Havenstreet
18. NEWPORT — arr
19. — dep
20. Medina Wharf
21. Gas Works Siding
22. Mill Hill
23. COWES — arr
24.

C8 — SATURDAYS

DOWN — Ryde, Sandown, Ventnor, Newport and Cowes

(DOWN timetable; three panels of departure/arrival columns)

Stations (rows):

1. PORTSMOUTH Hbr. }Boat — dep
2. RYDE PIER — dep
3. RYDE PIER HEAD — dep
4. Esplanade
5. St. John's Road
6. Smallbrook Jn.
7. Brading — arr
8. — dep
9. Sandown — arr
10. — dep
11. Shanklin — arr
12. — dep
13. Wroxall — arr
14. — dep
15. VENTNOR — arr
16. Ashey
17. Havenstreet
18. NEWPORT — arr
19. — dep
20. Medina Wharf
21. Gas Works Siding
22. Mill Hill
23. COWES — arr
24.

WHITSUN HOLIDAY ARRANGEMENTS, 1962.

CARRIAGE STOCK WORKINGS.

WHIT-SUNDAY, 10TH JUNE. (S.T.S.)

TRAIN 'F'.
6-coach set.

p.m.		p.m.
7A 4	R	7†45
7†50	SJ	–

TRAIN 'J'.
3-coach set.

p.m.		p.m.
8A 9	R	8.30
9.14	C	9.24
9.35	N	–

WHIT-MONDAY, 11TH JUNE. (W.T.S.)

TRAIN 'A'.
6-coach set.

p.m.		p.m.
2A21	R	3. 5
3.54	V	4.22
5. 3	R	5.25
6.10	V	6.42
7.21	R	8.18
8.59	C	9. 6
9.17	N	
For cleaning.		

TRAIN 'B'.
6-coach set.

p.m.		p.m.
1A21	R	2. 5
2.54	V	3.22
4. 3	R	4.25
5.10	V	5.42
6.21	R	6†45
6†50	SJ	–

TRAIN 'C'.
6-coach set.

a.m.		a.m.
	SJ	10†45
10.50	R	11. 5
11.54	V	12.22
1. 3	R	1.25
2.10	V	2.42
3.21	R	4. 5
4.54	V	5.22
6. 3	R	6.25
	etc.	

TRAIN 'D'.
6-coach set.

p.m.		p.m.
12A21	R	1. 5
1.54	V	2.22
3. 2	R	3.25
4.10	V	4.42
5.21	R	5†45
5†50	SJ	–

TRAIN 'G'.
6-coach set.

a.m.		a.m.
	SJ	11†45
11.50	R	12. 5
12.54	V	1.22
2. 3	R	2.25
3.10	V	3.42
4.21	R	5. 5
5.54	V	6.22
7. 3	R	7.25
	etc.	

GUARDS' ROSTERS.
WHIT-MONDAY, 11TH JUNE.

RYDE DEPOT.

No. 6 Pass.

p.m.		p.m.
On duty		1.41
	SJ	1.56
2. 3	R	2A18

No. 4 Goods.

a.m.		a.m.
On duty		5.30
	SJ	5‖50
6‖20	V	6A35
7A13	R	
	SJ	10†45
10†50	R	11. 5
11.54	V	12.22
1. 3	R	1.18Asst
1.24	SJ	–
Off duty 1.30pm.		

No. 9 Goods.

p.m.		p.m.
On duty		2.40
	SJ	2‖45
2‖50	R	3. 5
3.54	V	4.22
5. 3	R	5†45
5†50	SJ	–
–	SJ	9A43

No. 7 Goods.

p.m.		p.m.
On duty		12.40
	SJ	12‖45
12‖50	R	1. 5
1.54	V	2.22
3. 3	R	4. 5
4.54	V	5.22
6. 3	R	6†45
6†50	SJ	–
Off duty 8.40pm.		

No. 10 Goods.

a.m.		a.m.
On duty		6.15
	SJ	6‖25
7‖ 5	C	7A26
until		
10A32	SJ	11†45
11†50	R	12. 5
12.54	V	1.22
1.55	SJ	–
Off duty 2.10pm.		

NEWPORT DEPOT.

No. 2 Goods.

p.m.		p.m.
On duty		12.40
	N	12.46 Asst.
1.13	R	2. 5
2.54	V	3.22
4. 3	R	5. 5
5.54	V	6.22
7. 3	R	7.18 Asst.
7.45	N	–
Off duty 8.40pm.		

A – NORMAL WORKING.

NEWPORT A.D.M.O.
25. 5. 62.

Cowes Fireworks, August 1962

SOUTHERN REGION. L.(W) DISTRICT.   SPECIAL NOTICE NO. 43. L.W.D. (I.W.).
NEWPORT, I.W.   19TH JULY, 1961.

(1)   F R I D A Y, 4TH A U G U S T - C O W E S F I R E W O R K S.

ADDITIONAL WORKING :-

	PASS.		PASS.		L.E.			ECS.	PASS.	
	arr.	dep.	arr.	dep.					arr.	arr.	dep.
	p.m.	p.m.	p.m.	p.m.	mdt.				p.m.	p.m.	p.m.
COWES		10.35		10.47		RYDE ST.JOHN'S	9†20				11.25
Mill Hill				10.49½		Smallbrook Jn.	9.23			11.28	
NEWPORT	10.45	10.48	10.58	11. 0		Brading				11.33	11.34
Havenstreet		10.58½		11.10½		Sandown				11.38	11.39
Ashey		11. 3		11.15		Shanklin				11.44	11.45
VENTNOR					12‖ 5	Wroxall				11.53	11.54
Wroxall					12.10	VENTNOR				11.59	
Shanklin					12.15	Havenstreet	9.31				
Sandown					12.19	Newport	9.40				
Brading					12.23	COWES	9†50				
Smallbrook Jn.		11. 7		11.19	12.28	Stock		10.47		Berth.	
RYDE ST.JOHN'S	11. 9		11.21		12‖30	form :-		Up.			
To form :		11.25pm		Berth.							
		Ventnor.									

10†25pm Cowes to Ryde St.John's will not run.
10‖32pm Ventnor to Ryde St.John's will be ECS.

ALTERATIONS TO ENGINE DUTIES AND CARRIAGE STOCK WORKINGS.

ENGINE DUTIES

arr. NO.3(0.2Class) dep.			arr. NO.5(02.Class) dep.		
p.m.		p.m.	p.m.		p.m.
7‖21A	RSJ	7‖25	10A17	C	10.47
7‖30	LOCO	8‖45	11.21	RSJ	-
8‖50	RSJ	9†20	Normal rosters.		
9‖30	C	10.35			
11. 9	RSJ	11.25			
11.59	V	12‖ 5			
12‖30am	RSJ	-			

ADDTNL. SET ON 6. OPM.

A - NORMAL WORKING.

CARRIAGE STOCK WORKINGS.

TRAIN 'A'. 6-coach set.		TRAIN 'C'. 6-coach set.	
p.m.	p.m.	p.m.	p.m.
10A24	V	10†32	8A21	R	9.35
10†58	SJ	-	10.17	C	10.35
			11. 9 SJ	11.25

TRAIN 'I'. 4-coach set.	
a.m.	
9A50 SJ	p.m.
p.m. SJ	9†20
9†50	C	10.47
11.21 SJ	-

11.59 V -
Form train 'B' Saturday.

TRAIN 'H'.
4-coach set.
p.m.   p.m.
9A 9 R Berth.
Form train 'I' Saturday.

(2)   SATURDAY, 5TH AUGUST - LEICESTER AND LOUGHBORO' TOWN HOLIDAYS.
         Portsmouth Harbour arr. 3.48am and 4.20am.
ADDITIONAL WORKING.

	ECS.			PASS.	
	a.m.			arr. a.m.	dep. a.m.
RYDE ST.JOHN'S	6†10	RYDE PIER HEAD			6.40
RYDE PIER HEAD	6†15	RYDE ST.JOHN'S		6.45	6B46

B - AS BOOKED.

ALTERATIONS TO ENGINE DUTY, CARRIAGE STOCK WORKINGS AND GUARD'S ROSTER.

ENGINE DUTY NO. 6.		TRAIN 'A'. 6-set. a.m.		TRAIN 'C'. 6-set. a.m.		TRAIN 'I'. 4-set. a.m.		NO. 3 PASS. GUARD.
LOCO.	5‖55am	a.m. SJ	6†15	a.m. SJ	6†10	R	7. 7	On duty 5.55am
6‖0am RSJ	6†10	6†20 R	8A55	6†15 R	6.40			SJ 6†10
6†15	R	6.40						6†15 R 6.40
7‖20	V	7‖37						

Shedmen prepare A.
1st set on 5.40am.

A - NORMAL WORKING.

FOR DETAILS OF 'Q' TRAINS AT 6.55PM AND 7.45PM FROM RYDE PIER HEAD TO VENTNOR
SEE SPECIAL NOTICE NO. 42 L.W.D.(I.W.)

Ryde Carnival, September 1961

SOUTHERN REGION. L.(W) DISTRICT.　　　　SPECIAL NOTICE NO. 51. L.W.D.(I.W.).
NEWPORT, I.W.　　　　　　　　　　　　　　31ST AUGUST, 1961.

(1)　　　　　RYDE CARNIVAL　-　THURSDAY, 7TH SEPTEMBER.

SPECIAL TRAINS WILL RUN AS UNDER :-

Formed of :-	7†10pm ex N. PASS.		6.40pm ex V. PASS.		8†30pm ex SJ PASS.		7.40pm ex V. PASS.		9.40pm ex V. PASS.		9†54pm ex C. PASS.	
	arr. p.m.	dep. p.m.	arr. p.m.	dep. p.m.	arr. p.m.	dep. p.m.	arr. p.m.	dep. p.m.	arr. p.m.	dep. p.m.	arr. p.m.	dep. p.m.
RYDE P.HD.		7.53		8. 2		8.53		9. 2		10.44		10.50
Ryde Esp.	7.55	8. 0	8. 4	8. 9	8.55	9. 0	9. 4	9. 9	10.46	10.48	10.52	10.54
RYDE ST.JN	8. 3	8. 6	8.12	8.13	9. 3	9. 6	9.12	9.13	10.51	10.53	10.57	11. 0
Smallbk.Jn	8. 9		8.16		9. 9		9.16		10.56		11. 3	
Brading			8.21	8.22			9.21	9.22			11. 8	11. 9
Sandown			8.26	8.28			9.26	9.28			11.13	11.15
Shanklin			8.33	8.36			9.33	9.36			11.20	11.22
Wroxall			8.44	8X47			9.44	9X47			11.30	11.31
VENTNOR			8.52				9.52				11.36	
Ashey		8.13				9.13				11. 0		
Havenst.		8.18				9.18				11X 5		
NEWPORT	8.27	8.36				9.27	9.36			11.14	11.16	
Mill Hill		8.45					9.45				11.25	
COWES	8.47					9.47				11.27		

	ECS	7.20pmFt RETIMED		ECS.		ECS.	ECS.		ECS.		ECS.	
	p.m.	p.m.	p.m.	arr. p.m.	dep. p.m.	p.m.	arr. p.m.	dep. p.m.	arr. p.m.	dep. p.m.	arr. p.m.	dep. p.m.
COWES						8†52				9†54		
NEWPORT	7†10					9† 2		9†40	10† 4	10† 6		
Havenst.	7.20					9X50	10. 0		10.16			
VENTNOR			7.15		9† 0						10†10	
Wroxall				9X 5							10X15	10.20
Shanklin				9.11							10.25	
Sandown				9.15							10.29	
Brading		7.33	7.45	9.19	9.23						10.33	
Smallbk.Jn	7.28		7.51	9.28			10.13		10.24		10.38	
RYDE ST.JN	7L30	7.54		9†30			10†15					
RYDE P.HD.	7†35								10†31		10†45	
Disposal :	7C53			Berth.			Berth.		10V50		Berth.	

	7. 0pmFt RETIMED	ECS.	ECS.	L.E.
	p.m.	p.m.	p.m.	mdt.
COWES		11†35		
NEWPORT	10.20	11†45		12‖ 0
Havenst.	10.33			12.10
VENTNOR			11†44	
Wroxall			11.49	
Shanklin			11.55	
Sandown			11.59	
Brading			12. 3	
Smallbk.Jn	10.46		12. 8	12.18
RYDE ST.JN	10.50		12†10	12‖20

IN THE EVENT OF THE CARNIVAL BEING POSTPONED, THE SPECIAL LATE TRAINS WILL NOT RUN.

L - Stop only to change Enginemen.

7†45pm Ryde St.John's to Ryde Pier Head. Additional, arr. 7†50pm (Form 8.25pm Down).
8.25pm Ryde Pier Head to Ventnor. Retimed dep. Wroxall 9X 7pm, arr. Ventnor 9.12pm.
8†30pm (4-set) Ryde St.John's to Ryde Pier Head. Addtnl., arr. 8†35pm (Form 8.53pm Down).
8‖45pm Ryde St.John's to Ryde Pier Head. Addtnl., arr. 8‖50pm.
9.40pm Ventnor to Ryde St.John's Road. Extended empty to Ryde Pier Head, arr. 10†18pm.
10‖ 5pm Newport to Ryde St.John's Rd. Will not run.
10‖30pm Cowes to Ryde St.John's. Retimed : dep.Havenstreet 11X 7, Smallbrook Jn. 11/15,
　　　　　　　　　　　　　　　　　　　　　　　　　　Ryde St.John's Road arr. 11‖17pm.

11‖ 0pm Ryde Pier Head to Ryde St.John's. Additional, arr. 11‖ 5pm.

NOTE AND ADVISE ALL CONCERNED.　　　　　　　　H. E. BARBER,
　　　　　　　　　　　　　　　　　　DISTRICT TRAFFIC SUPERINTENDENT.
　　　　　　　　　　　　　　　　　　　　　　per : -

BRITISH   RAILWAYS
Southern Region

RYDE CARNIVAL - THURSDAY, 7TH SEPTEMBER, 1961

Referring to Special Notice No. 51 . L.W.D.(I.W.), the following alterations to Engine Duties and Carriage Stock Workings will apply : -

ENGINE   DUTIES

NO. 2.		
p.m.		p.m.
9Λ35	N	9†40
10†15	RSJ	—

3rd set on 4Λ58pm,
Change with 2nd set
of No. 7 @ R. 5.45pm.
Disposal by 5. 0pm ΛO.men.

NO. 3.		
p.m.		p.m.
6†45Λ	RSJ	6‖55
7‖0	LOCO	8‖10
8‖15	RSJ	8†30
8†35	R	8.53
9.47	C	9†54
10†31	R	10.44
11.27	C	11†35
11†45	N	12‖0mdt
12‖20am	RSJ	—

2nd set on 12Λ10pm,
Rlf. 7.55pm by
3rd set (Addtnl) on 6. 0pm
Λ.O. and above.

NO. 4.		
p.m.		p.m.
5†50Λ	RSJ	6‖0
6‖5	LOCO	7‖25
7‖30	RSJ	7†45
7†50	R	8.25
9.12	V	9.40
10.11	RSJ	10†13
10†18	R	10.50
11.36	V	11†44
12†10am	RSJ	—

2nd set on 11Λ17am.
Rlf. 7. 0pm by
3rd set (Addtnl) on
5.30pm.Λ.O. & above.

NO. 5.		
p.m.		p.m.
10Λ17	C	10‖30Λ
11‖17	RSJ	

Usual rosters.

NO. 8.		
p.m.		p.m.
7Λ21	R	7.53
8.47	C	8†52
9†2	N	Ft.10.20
10.50	RSJ	—

2nd set on 2Λ58pm,
Disposal by 5. 0pm
ΛO.men.

NO. 6.
Normal working and rosters,
but 2nd set on 1Λ58pm to
dispose of own engine.

NO. 9.
Normal working and rosters,
but 2nd set on 3Λ30pm to
dispose of own engine.

NO. 11.		
p.m.		p.m.
Λ	N	7†10
7†35	R	8. 2
8.52	V	9†0
9†30	RSJ	—

2nd set on 11Λ23am, Rlf.
7.30pm Up by 5. 0pm
Λ.O.men who also
dispose of Nos. 2 & 8.

NO. 7.		
p.m.		p.m.
6Λ52	V	Ft.7.15
7.54	RSJ	8‖45
8‖50	R	9. 2
9.52	V	10†10
10†45	R	11‖0
11‖5	RSJ	—

2nd set on 1Λ45pm,
Change with 3rd set
of No. 2 @ R. 5.45pm.

CARRIAGE   STOCK   WORKINGS.

TRAIN 'B'.		
p.m.		p.m.
7Λ21	R	8. 2
8.52	V	9†0
9†30	SJ	—

TRAIN 'C'.		
p.m.		p.m.
8Λ21	R	9. 2
9.52	V	10†10
10†45	R	—

TRAIN 'F'.		
p.m.		p.m.
Λ6†45	SJ	7†45
7†50	R	8.25
9.12	V	9.40
10.11	SJ	10†13
10†18	R	10.44%%%
11.27	C	11†35
11†45	N	—

TRAIN 'I'.		
a.m.		p.m.
Λ9†50	SJ	8†30
8†35	R	8.53
9.47	C	9†54
10†31	R	10.50
11.36	V	11†44
12†10	SJ	—

TRAIN 'J'.		
p.m.		p.m.
8Λ9	R	8.30
9.14	C	9.24
9.35	N	9†40
10†15	SJ	—

TRAIN 'K'.		
p.m.		p.m.
	N	7†10
7†35	R	7.53
8.47	C	8†52
9†2	N	—

Λ - Normal working.
%%% - Detach 2 coaches at Newport.

NEWPORT. A.D.T.S.O.
31. 8. 61.

Appendix Four – Tank Traps on the Isle of Wight Railways

by Jimmy E. James

In the early part of the Second World War, after all the station nameplates had been removed on the Isle of Wight railways, work of a more serious nature followed. Tank traps were designed and sited at strategic points throughout the Island railway system. Nine separate locations were selected as follows:

a. Wroxall end of Ventnor Tunnel.
b. Thirty yards north of Morton Common bridge between Brading and Sandown. Two were positioned here, on the 'down' line and one on the 'up' line.
c. Blackwater side of Shide station.
d. Ryde end of Newport Tunnel.
e. Newport end of Gunville bridge, on the Freshwater line.
f. Cowes side of the Cement Mills Viaduct.
g. Close to Freshwater Causeway Crossing gates.
h. St Lawrence end of Whitwell Tunnel, on the Ventnor West branch.

My first job was to make all the templates and levelling boards which were necessary for positioning all the concrete blocks in their correct locations. The composition of each tank trap layout consisted of two large pre-cast concrete blocks, approximately ten feet long, too feet wide and four feet deep, with eight pre-cast blocks eighteen inches square and four feet deep. All these were sunk into the ground in the centre of the track, to a planned layout, so that the top surface was level with the top of the sleepers. In each of the blocks was an aperture designed to hold a standard rail metal and specially bent metals would be inserted when the blocks were in position, when and if, the situation arose.

I was present on the construction site of each tank trap and I can remember clearly the feelings of my colleagues at the time, 'this was not railway work, it was something which had an entirely different meaning'. Sunday was chosen for the day when the first railway tank trap would be constructed quite close to Shide Crossing gates on the Blackwater side. The works train consisted of an engineers work van, three flat bolster wagons with the precast blocks, the mobile crane from Ryde St John's Road, one with an Engineers' Department supply of equipment aboard, and a guard's van. As we were feeling our way, so to speak, the layout at Shide was only half completed by 5 o'clock and we had to complete the job the following Sunday. The same thing happened just north of the Cement Mills Viaduct, as again it took us two Sundays to complete.

The powers that be then decided on a new approach. At the Ryde end of Newport Tunnel all the excavations were made between the sleepers during the week, with the object in view of completing a whole layout in one day. As you may gather, all the trains had to be cancelled when these operations were in progress as the track had to be broken. On this day the first scheduled train was timed to leave Newport station for Ryde Pier Head at 6.15pm. It so happened that it rained nearly all day and as excavations were in clay and hard gravel, the whole site was a quagmire. I think that this was the hardest day's work that the whole staff involved in the tank trap project had ever had. Incidentally, the number of men present was approximately twenty. We did complete this layout however in one day, although it was nearly dark when the works train left the site and I recall we all had to scramble onto it wherever we could. I know that I managed to climb aboard the crane, but even so we delayed the departure of the Ryde train for some thirty minutes.

Again the site at Gunville was prepared as much as possible during the week, but after what we had learned from the previous layouts this one was completed fairly comfortably in one day. The same was so with the Freshwater Causeway tank trap the following week, although we did have to get the services of a plumber because of a burst water pipe.

The sites on the 'up' and 'down' lines at Morton Common on the main line between Brading and Sandown were the easiest of the lot because the digging was mostly sand and the weather on both weekends was perfect. Ventnor Tunnel tank trap was a different proposition, the digging was hard, consisting of stones of every shape and size, although it was completed in one day. The final layout a week later was on the St Lawrence site of Whitwell Tunnel and although work was carried out during the week the excavation through hard stone was nowhere near complete. After a very hard Sunday of, 'blood, sweat and toil', to use Winston Churchill's words, only 75% of the layout was completed. The three smaller blocks had to be sited on the following week and it was decided to leave the whole works train behind. The staff travelled to the site by coach and completed the job with manpower alone.

When each layout was completed the metals were placed in position to prove their accuracy and then taken out and laid close at hand. The whole operation took some twelve to thirteen weeks, and all the necessary rail metals were left at each site to be put into their emergency positions if required. Although I walked over these sites many, many times in the ensuing years, I cannot in any way recall if the concrete blocks were ever removed, or whether they are still in position.

Fortunately the tank traps were never manned in an emergency. Looking back now it seems to have been a complete waste of time, effort and money. Who could visualise German tanks landing in the hilly Ventnor district, and eventually finding themselves going through Ventnor Tunnel, or, Whitwell Tunnel? If the German army had landed at Cowes, and assuming they got by the Cement Mills trap, how would they have traversed a narrow viaduct restricted by a weight limit? Personally I could not visualise the German invading forces using any rail track, but I support that the Isle of Wight had to be included in an overall defence plan.

Tank Trap layouts sited on the Isle of Wight railway system, 1940.

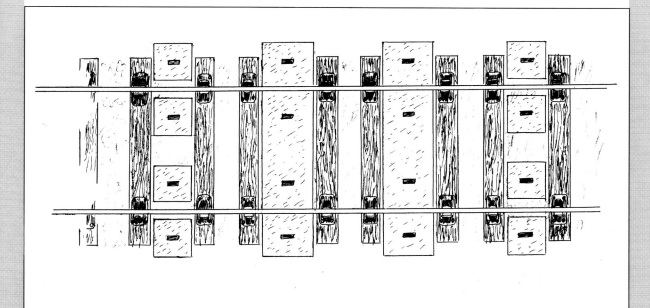

Plan of the Tank Trap layout

Elevation

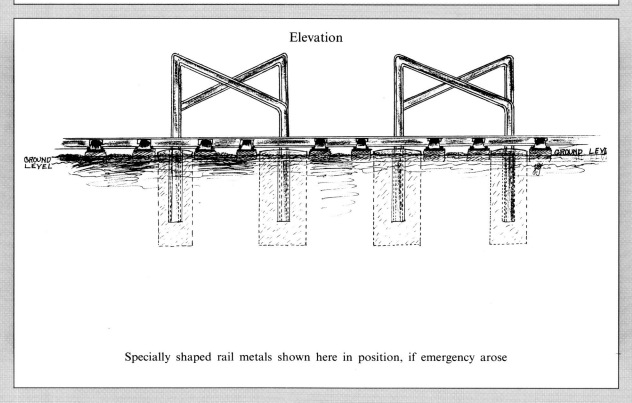

GROUND LEVEL

GROUND LEVEL

Specially shaped rail metals shown here in position, if emergency arose

Appendix Five – Summary of Southern Railway rolling stock and passenger train set formations

Rolling Stock

Bogie Coaches
LBSCR	60
LCDR	39
IWCR	1
	100

4-wheeled Coaches
LCDR	3

Bogie Guard's Vans
LSWR	9
LCDR	2
	11

4-wheeled Guard's Vans
LSWR	1
LCDR	1
	2

4-wheeled Horse Box
LBSCR	1

4-wheeled Open Carriage Truck 1

Ryde Pier Tramway
Drewry Petrol Cars	2
Trailer Cars	2
Luggage Trailer	1
	5

Total Vehicles 123

Number of Set Trains 20

Wagon Stock
Open Goods	449
Covered Vans	51
Rail Timber Single Bolster	20

Highway Vehicle Flats	15
Service Vehicles:	
2-ton Crane	1
5-Ton Crane	1
10-Ton Crane	1
Match Trucks	2
Tool Vans	4
Boiler Truck	1
Tank Truck	1
Weed Killing Tanks	2
Weed Killing Brake Van	1
Tar Tanks	2
Cattle Wagons	3
Ballast Wagons	20
CME and Loco	12
Goods Brakes	13

Total Vehicles 599

Set Trains

Set No. (and Depot)	Coach	Description and Origin		Compartments	Seating Capacity 1st	Seating Capacity 3rd	Overall Dimensions	Weight Tons
489 (R)	4155	3rd Bke	C	6		60	57′ 7″ x 8′ 10″	24
	4156	3rd Bke	C	6		60	57′ 7″ x 8′ 10″	24
	6362	Compo.	C	7	24	40	50′ 11″ x 8′ 10″	21
	6363	Compo.	C	7	24	40	50′ 11″ x 8′ 10″	23
	2410	3rd	C	8		80	51′ 7″ x 8′ 10″	21
	2411	3rd	C	8		80	50′ 11″ x 8′ 10″	21
490 (R)	4170	3rd Bke	C	4		40	57′ 7″ x 8′ 10″	25
	4173	3rd Bke	C	7		70	57′ 7″ x 8′ 10″	26
	2423+	3rd	E	8		80	49′ 8″ x 8′ 11″	21
	6344	Compo.	C	8	24	50	57′ 7″ x 8′ 10″	26
	6394*	Compo.	E	7	24	40	49′ 8″ x 8′ 11″	21
491 (R)	4171	3rd Bke	C	4		40	57′ 7″ x 8′ 10″	25
	4174	3rd Bke	C	7		70	57′ 7″ x 8′ 10″	26
	6345	Compo.	C	8	24	50	57′ 7″ x 8′ 10″	26
	6395*	Compo.	E	7	24	40	49′ 6″ x 8′ 11″	21
	2422+	3rd	E	8		80	49′ 6″ x 8′ 11″	21
492 (R)	4172	3rd Bke	C	4		40	57′ 7″ x 8′ 10″	24
	4175	3rd Bke	C	7		70	57′ 7″ x 8′ 10″	26
	6346	Compo.	C	8	24	50	57′ 7″ x 8′ 10″	26
	6396*	Compo.	E	7	24	40	48′ 6″ x 8′ 11″	21
	2421+	3rd	E	8		80	49′ 6″ x 8′ 11″	21
493 (R)	4109*	3rd Bke	E	5		50	49′ 6″ x 8′ 11″	20
	4117	3rd Bke	E	7		70	49′ 8″ x 8′ 10″	21
	2427+	3rd	E	8		80	49′ 6″ x 8′ 11″	21
	2428+	3rd	E	8		80	49′ 8″ x 8′ 10″	21
	6359	Compo.	E	6	24	30	43′ 8″ x 8′ 10″	19
	6397*	Compo.	E	7	24	40	48′ 6″ x 8′ 11″	21

Set No. (and Depot)	Coach	Description and Origin		Compart- ments	Seating Capacity 1st	3rd	Overall Dimensions	Weight Tons
494 (R)	4161	3rd Bke	C	7		70	57′ 7″ x 8′ 10″	24
	2430	3rd	E	8		80	49′ 6″ x 8′ 11″	21
	2431	3rd	E	8		80	49′ 6″ x 8′ 10″	21
	2436	3rd	E	7		70	45′ 8″ x 8′ 10″	20
497 (R)	4141*	3rd Bke	W	7		70	51′ 8″ x 8′ 11″	23
	2418	3rd	E	7		70	43′ 8″ x 8′ 11″	19
	2419	3rd	E	7		70	43′ 8″ x 8′ 10″	19
	2420	3rd	E	7		70	43′ 8″ x 8′ 11″	19
	6358	Compo.	E	6	24	30	43′ 8″ x 8′ 11″	19
	6385+	Compo.	W	7	24	40	49′ 8″ x 8′ 11″	21
500 (R)	4162	3rd Bke	C	6		60	57′ 7″ x 8′ 10″	24
	2407	3rd	C	9		90	57′ 7″ x 8′ 10″	24
	6348	Compo.	C	8	24	50	57′ 7″ x 8′ 10″	26
	6349	Compo.	C	8	24	50	57′ 7″ x 8′ 10″	26
	1012	Gds Van	E				48′ 8″ x 8′ 11″	19
502 (R) Bembge. Branch	4168	3rd Bke	C	5		50	57′ 7″ x 8′ 10″	25
	2437	3rd	E	7		70	45′ 8″ x 8′ 10″	20
	6347	Compo.	C	8	24	50	57′ 7″ x 8′ 10″	26
Loose (R)	2404 (490)	3rd	C	9		90	57′ 7″ x 8′ 10″	26
	2405 (491)	3rd	C	9		90	57′ 7″ x 8′ 10″	25
	2406 (500)	3rd	C	9		90	57′ 7″ x 8′ 10″	24
	2412 (492)	3rd	C	9		90	57′ 7″ x 8′ 10″	20
	2413	3rd	C	9		90	57′ 7″ x 8′ 10″	21
	2429	3rd	E	8		80	49′ 6″ x 8′ 11″	21
Guard's Vans	1003	4-w	W				33′ 7″ x 9′ 0″	12
	1008	4-w	E				31′ 6″ x 8′ 10″	11
	1014	Bogie	W				47′ 7″ x 9′ 1″	19
	1015	Bogie	W				47′ 7″ x 9′ 1″	19
	1020	Bogie	W				47′ 7″ x 9′ 1″	19
	1021	Bogie	W				47′ 7″ x 9′ 1″	19
	1022	Bogie	W				47′ 7″ x 9′ 1″	19
	1023	Bogie	W				47′ 7″ x 9′ 1″	19
Mail	4124	3rd Bke 4-w	E	2		20	33′ 6″ x 8′ 10″	11
	4133	3rd Bke 4-w	E	2		20	33′ 6″ x 8′ 10″	11
485 (N)	4151	3rd Bke	C	6		60	57′ 7″ x 8′ 10″	24
	4157	3rd Bke	C	7		70	57′ 7″ x 8′ 10″	26
	6353	Compo.	C	8	24	50	57′ 7″ x 8′ 10″	26
486 (N)	4152	3rd Bke	C	6		60	57′ 7″ x 8′ 10″	24
	4158	3rd Bke	C	7		70	57′ 7″ x 8′ 10″	26
	6354	Compo.	C	8	24	50	57′ 7″ x 8′ 10″	26
487 (N)	4153	3rd Bke	C	6		60	57′ 7″ x 8′ 10″	24
	4159	3rd Bke	C	7		70	57′ 7″ x 8′ 10″	26
	6355	Compo.	C	8	24	50	57′ 7″ x 8′ 10″	26
488 (N)	4154	3rd Bke	C	6		60	57′ 7″ x 8′ 10″	24
	4160	3rd Bke	C	7		70	57′ 7″ x 8′ 10″	26
	6356	Compo.	C	8	24	50	57′ 7″ x 8′ 10″	26
495 (N)	4113	3rd Bke	E	5		50	48′ 8″ x 8′ 10″	20
	4114	3rd Bke	E	5		50	48′ 8″ x 8′ 10″	20
	2432	3rd	E	7		70	45′ 8″ x 8′ 10″	20
	6399	Compo.	E	7	24	40	48′ 8″ x 8′ 10″	21

Set No. (and Depot)	Coach	Description and Origin		Compart- ments	Seating Capacity 1st	Seating Capacity 3rd	Overall Dimensions	Weight Tons
496 (N)	4115	3rd Bke	E	5		50	48′ 8″ x 8′ 10″	20
	4116	3rd Bke	E	5		50	48′ 8″ x 8′ 10″	20
	2433	3rd	E	7		70	45′ 8″ x 8′ 10″	20
	6360	Compo.	E	7	24	40	48′ 8″ x 8′ 10″	21
498 (N)	4118	3rd Bke	C	6		60	57′ 7″ x 8′ 10″	24
	4121	3rd Bke	C	6		60	57′ 7″ x 8′ 10″	24
	2434	3rd	E	7		70	45′ 8″ x 8′ 10″	20
	6388	Compo.	E	7	24	40	48′ 8″ x 8′ 10″	21
499 (N)	4122	3rd Bke	C	6		60	57′ 7″ x 8′ 10″	24
	4123	3rd Bke	C	6		60	57′ 7″ x 8′ 10″	24
	2435	3rd	E	7		70	45′ 8″ x 8′ 10″	20
	6400	Compo.	E	7	24	40	48′ 8″ x 8′ 10″	21
P&P 503 (N) Merstone Branch	4169	3rd Bke	C	7		56	57′ 7″ x 8′ 10″	27
	6367	Compo.	C	9	19	37	57′ 7″ x 8′ 10″	27
	6987	Compo. Bke	C	7	12	40	57′ 7″ x 8′ 10″	27
506 (N)	4163	3rd Bke	C	6		60	57′ 7″ x 8′ 10″	24
	4164	3rd Bke	C	6		60	57′ 7″ x 8′ 10″	24
	6350	Compo.	C	8	24	50	57′ 7″ x 8′ 10″	26
507 (N)	4165	3rd Bke	C	6		60	57′ 7″ x 8′ 10″	24
	4166	3rd Bke	C	6		60	57′ 7″ x 8′ 10″	24
	6357	Compo.	C	8	24	50	57′ 7″ x 8′ 10″	26
Loose (N) (506)	2408	3rd	C	9		90	57′ 7″ x 8′ 10″	24
(507)	2409	3rd	C	9		90	57′ 7″ x 8′ 10″	24
(488)	2414	3rd	C	9		90	57′ 7″ x 8′ 10″	24
(485)	2415	3rd	C	9		90	57′ 7″ x 8′ 10″	24
(486)	2416	3rd	C	9		90	57′ 7″ x 8′ 10″	24
(487)	2417	3rd	C	9		90	57′ 7″ x 8′ 10″	24
	2424	3rd	E	8		80	49′ 6″ x 8′ 11″	21
	2425	3rd	E	8		80	49′ 6″ x 8′ 11″	21
	2426	3rd	E	8		80	49′ 6″ x 8′ 11″	21
	4103	3rd Bke	IWC	4		46	48′ 2″ x 8′ 11″	20
	6986	Compo.	C	4	11	48	57′ 7″ x 8′ 10½″	26
Mail (N)	4150	3rd Bke 4-w	E	2		20	33′ 6″ x 8′ 10″	11
Guards Vans (N)	1017	Bogie	W				47′ 7″ x 9′ 1″	19
	1018	Bogie	W				47′ 7″ x 9′ 1″	19
	1019	Bogie	W				47′ 7″ x 9′ 1″	19
Boat Truck	4381	Conv. underframe ex-E					33′ 6″ x 8′ 0″	7½
Horse Box	3370	4-w	C	1		5	17′ 0″ x 8′ 0″	7

Notes
(N) – Newport Depot
(R) – Ryde Depot
C – Ex-LBSCR
E – Ex-LCDR
W – Ex-LSWR
* – Dynamo
+ – Wired